Take a Hike!

Family Walks in the Rochester Area

RICH and SUE FREEMAN

Take a Hike!
Family Walks in the Rochester Area

RICH and SUE FREEMAN

Footprint Press

PO Box 645, Fishers, NY 14453
http://www.footprintpress.com

Other books available from Footprint Press:

*Take A Hike! Family Walks in the Finger Lakes
    & Genesee Valley Region*
Take Your Bike! Family Rides in the Rochester Area
*Take Your Bike! Family Rides in the Finger Lakes
    & Genesee Valley Region*
Bruce Trail – An Adventure Along the Niagara Escarpment
*Peak Experiences – Hiking the Highest Summits of New York,
    County by County*
Alter – A Simple Path to Emotional Wellness

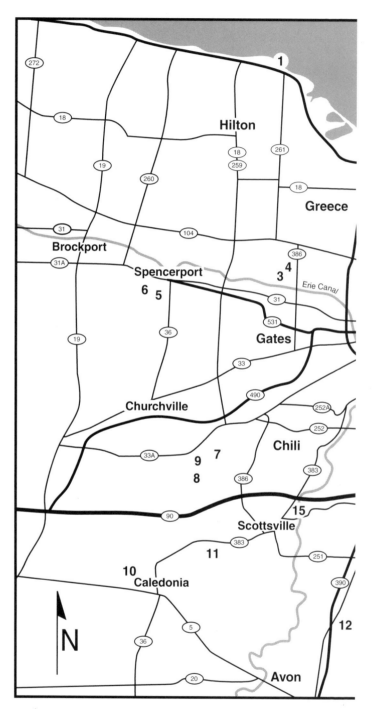

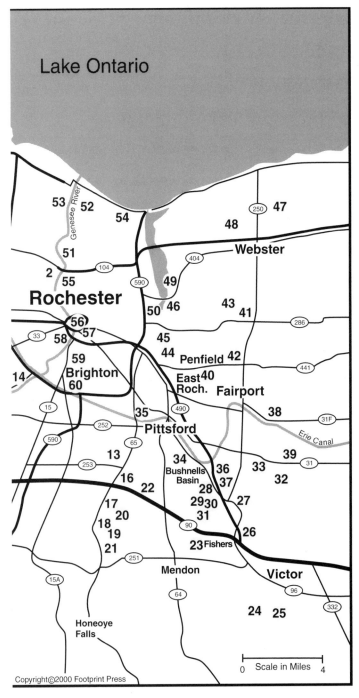

Lake Ontario

Genesee River

53 52
54

51
2
55

Rochester

56
57
58
59
Brighton
60

14

15

33

104

590

50 46
45
44 Penfield 42

East 40
Roch.

35
252
Pittsford

65

590

13

253

16
22

17
18 20
19
21

251

15A

Honeoye
Falls

250 47
48
Webster

404

49

43 41

286

441

Fairport

490

38

31F

Erie Canal

39
33 32
34
Bushnells
Basin 36
28 37
29 30
31
23 Fishers
Mendon

90

31

27
26
Victor

24 25

64

96

332

0 Scale in Miles 4

Copyright©2000 Footprint Press

5

Contents

Contents

Walks Northeast of Rochester

Acknowledgements

The research, writing, production, and promotion of a book such as this is never a solitary adventure. *Take A Hike!* came into being because of the assistance of many wonderful people who freely shared their knowledge, experience, resources, thoughts, and time. We extend our heartfelt thanks to them all. Each in his or her own way is responsible for making the Rochester area a better place to live and, most of all, a community rich with the spirit of collaboration for the betterment of all. This is what ensures quality of life within a community. Thank you, each and every one.

Carol & John Aldridge, Tinker Nature Park
Robert Butler, Bluebird Haven Trail
Brenda Caine, Corn Hill resident
Alice Calabrese, Humane Society at Lollypop Farm
Allen Coletta, City of Rochester, Bureau of Parks & Recreation
Michael Cooper, Penfield Parks & Recreation
Jim Farr, City of Rochester, Bureau of Parks & Recreation
Dick Freitas, Penfield Trails
Fran Gotcsik, Genesee Valley Greenway
Eric Johnson, Monroe County Parks
Eileen Kennedy, Monroe County Parks
Jack Kerson, Friends of Webster Trails
Brendan Knaup, Monroe County Parks
Jerry Lavigne, Brighton Recreation and Parks
Jane Luce, Town of Victor
Joanne Mitchell, Greece Canal Park
Dave Rinaldo, Monroe County Parks
Mary Anna Russo, Helmer Nature Center
Dave Schaeffer, Crescent Trail Association
Joseph Schuler, Old Rifle Range Trail
Shirley Shaw, Thousand Acre Swamp Sanctuary
Dick Spade, Adirondack Mountain Club
George Turner, Webster Parks Department
Ron Walker, Hanson Nature Center
Dan Wilson, Adirondack Mountain Club
Dave Wright, Victor Hiking Trails

These people directed us to choice trails, reviewed our maps and descriptions, supplied historical tidbits, and often are responsible for the existence and maintenance of the trails. They have our sincere appreciation.

A special thanks to our cover models. John, Marie, Jeff, Corinne, and Melanie Green made a special trip and endured our "one more shot" ploys with patience and true friendship. Thanks.

Introduction

Wow, what a ride this has been. In 1997 we issued the original *Take A Hike!* book and wondered if the Rochester community would show any interest. We worked hard to get the word out and were rewarded with a warm reception. Our greatest thrill was at book signings when people would come up to us and glowingly describe how the book had inspired them, either solo or as part of a group, to begin an exercise program based on hiking each of the trails. Now that you've been inspired to begin, keep hiking. This book has 25 brand new trails to explore. All the trails have been rehiked, verified, and the maps redrawn.

If you're new to the Rochester area, there's no better way to learn your way around than by using this book as your guide. It will introduce you to our rich history and lead you to explore our diverse natural beauty.

Besides, taking a hike or a short walk is good for you. In as little as one hour you can do your body a favor – stretch your legs, raise your heart rate, and decrease your stress level. Hiking is a perfect exercise to balance today's hectic lifestyle.

Over the past years we have enjoyed hiking in many states throughout the United States. It didn't matter if it was a brief walk or extended backpacking trip. Every time we ventured outside, mother nature offered something new and wonderful. We learned it's not necessary to go far to reap these benefits. Rochester and the surrounding towns are a treasure trove of great walks. The geographic terrain varies greatly and wildlife is abundant. The city and towns have had the vision to create parks and save wetlands, many with trails. We've learned that the Rochester area is unique in its level of volunteerism in the establishment and maintenance of hiking trails. Few other cities have local trail groups like Rochester. The trail groups all welcome volunteers and new members. We encourage everyone to join and help build and preserve trails for future generations to enjoy.

Most trails listed in this book are free and open to the public. A few require a small admission fee or request a donation. They are clearly noted in the heading to each trail beside the term "Admission." You do not have to be a member of the sponsoring group to enjoy any of the trails.

If you find inaccurate information or substantially different conditions (after all, things do change), please send a note detailing your findings to:

Footprint Press, P.O. Box 645, Fishers, NY 14453
or e-mail us: rich@footprintpress.com

How To Use This Book

We have clustered the hikes into five groups using the city of Rochester as the core and working in a counter clockwise spiral from the northwest, around the city. All the walks are found in Monroe County or the northwest corner of Ontario County — the Rochester suburban area:

Walks Northwest of Rochester
Walks Southwest of Rochester
Walks Southeast of Rochester
Walks Northeast of Rochester
Walks in Central Rochester

An overall map showing the locations of all the trails can be found on pages 4 and 5.

There's a major hiking trail in Rochester that you won't find in this book. The Erie Canalway Trail runs for 85 miles from Lockport to Palmyra and is used year-round by walkers, bikers, joggers, in-line skaters, and cross-country skiers. Maps and trail descriptions for this trail can be found in *Take Your Bike! Family Rides in the Rochester Area.*

Where possible, we have designated hikes that go in a loop to let you see as much as possible without backtracking. You can easily begin and end in one location and not worry about finding transportation back to the beginning. The indexes at the back list trails by a variety of criteria. Check them out to quickly zero in on trails that suit your purposes.

Approximate hiking times are given, but of course this depends on your speed. If you stop to watch the wildlife, enjoy the views, or read the descriptive plaques, it will take you longer than the time given. You'll notice that many of the hikes also have shortcuts or are connected to other trails that allow you to adjust your time on the trail.

The maps for each trail are just sketches. We wanted maps that were easy to view and understand so everyone could be comfortable looking at where they were going and what they were seeing. Some areas were never mapped for hiking trails prior to this book. On most of the maps, you'll find a small inset map. This gives a broader picture and lets you visually locate the trail relative to major towns and roads.

We found people were keeping notes in the margins of their original *Take A Hike!* books, so we've added a section at the end of each trail for you to log the date visited and any notes you may want to jot down about your experience on a specific trail.

Legend

At the beginning of each trail listing, you will find a map and description with the following information:

Location: The park, nature center, or town the trail is in.

Directions: How to find the trailhead parking area from a major road or town.

Alternative Parking: Other parking locations with access to the trail. Use these if you want to shorten your hike by starting or stopping at a spot other than the designated end-point.

Hiking Time: Approximate time to hike at a comfortable pace, including time to enjoy the views.

Length: The round-trip length of the hike in miles (unless noted as one-way).

Difficulty:

(1 boot) easy hiking, generally level trail

(2 boots) rolling hills, gradual grades on trail

(3 boots) gentle climbing required to follow the trail

(4 boots) some strenuous climbing required

Surface: The materials that make up the trail surface for the major portion of the hike.

Trail Markings: Markings used to designate the trails in this book vary widely. Some trails are not marked at all but can be followed by cleared or worn paths. This doesn't pose a problem for the hiker as long as there aren't many intersecting, unmarked paths. Other trails are well marked with either signs, blazes, or markers, and sometimes a combination of all three. Blazing is done by the official group that maintains the trail.

Signs – wooden or metal signs with instructions in words or pictures.

Blazes – painted markings on trees showing where the trail goes. Many blazes are rectangular and placed at eye level. (See the picture on page 127.) Colors may be used to denote different trails. If a tree has twin blazes beside one another, you should proceed cautiously because the trail either turns or another trail intersects.

Sometimes you'll see a section of trees with painted markings which aren't neat geometric shapes. These are probably boundary markers or trees marked for logging. Trail blazes are generally distinct geometric shapes and are placed at eye level.

Markers – small plastic or metal geometric shapes (square, round, triangular) nailed to trees at eye level to show where the trail goes. They also may be colored to denote different trails.

It is likely that at some point you will lose the blazes or markers while following a trail. The first thing to do is stop and look around. See if you can spot a blaze or marker by looking in all directions, including behind you. If not, backtrack until you see a blaze or marker, then proceed forward again, carefully following the markings.

Uses: Each trail has a series of icons depicting the activity or activities allowed on the trail. Jogging is allowed on all trails, as is snowshoeing when snow covers the ground. The icons include:

 Hiking

 Horseback Riding

 Bicycling

 Snowmobiling

 Cross-country Skiing

 Wheelchair Accessible

Contact: The address and phone number of the organization to contact if you would like additional information or if you have questions not answered in this book.

13

Map Legend

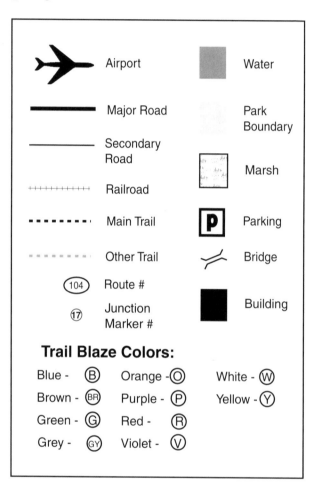

✈ Airport

Water

━━━━━ Major Road

Park Boundary

──────── Secondary Road

Marsh

++++++++++ Railroad

■ ■ ■ ■ ■ ■ Main Trail

P Parking

▪ ▪ ▪ ▪ ▪ Other Trail

Bridge

(104) Route #

⑰ Junction Marker #

Building

Trail Blaze Colors:

Blue - Ⓑ	Orange - Ⓞ	White - Ⓦ
Brown - ⓑⓡ	Purple - Ⓟ	Yellow - Ⓨ
Green - Ⓖ	Red - Ⓡ	
Grey - ⓖⓨ	Violet - Ⓥ	

Directions

In the directions we often tell you to turn left or right. To avoid confusion, in some instances we have noted a compass direction in parentheses according to the following:

(N) = north   (E) = east
(S) = south   (W) = west

Some trails have "Y" or "T" junctions. A "Y" junction indicates one path that turns into two paths. The direction we give is either bear left or bear right. A "T" junction is one path that ends at another. The direction is turn left or turn right.

Guidelines

Any adventure in the outdoors can be inherently dangerous. It's important to watch where you are going and keep an eye on children. Some of these trails are on private property where permission is benevolently granted by the landowners. Please respect the landowners and their property. Follow all regulations posted on signs and stay on the trails. Our behavior today will determine how many of these wonderful trails remain for future generations to enjoy.

Follow "no-trace" ethics whenever you venture outdoors. "No-trace" ethics means that the only thing left behind as evidence of your passing is your footprints. Carry out all trash you carry in. Do not litter. In fact, carry a plastic bag with you and pick up any litter you happen upon along the way. The trails included in this book are intended for day hikes. Please, no camping or fires.

As the trails age and paths become worn, trail work groups sometimes reroute the trails. This helps control erosion and allows vegetation to return. It also means that if a sign or marker doesn't appear as it is described in the book, it's probably because of trail improvement.

Remember:

Take only pictures, leave only footprints.
Please do not pick anything.

Preparations and Safety

You can enhance your time in the outdoors by dressing properly and carrying appropriate equipment. Even for a short day hike, take a small backpack or fanny pack with the following gear:

camera	flashlight
binoculars	insect repellent
compass	water bottle with water
rain gear	nature guidebook(s) of flowers, birds, etc.
snacks	plastic bag to pick up trash

Many of the trails can be muddy. It's best to wear lightweight hiking boots or at least sturdy sneakers.

Walking sticks have been around for centuries, but they are finding new life and new forms in recent years. These sticks can be anything from a branch picked up along the trail to a $200 pair of poles designed with built-in springs and hand-molded grips. Using a walking stick is a good idea, especially in hilly terrain. It can take the pressure off your knees and help you balance when crossing bridges or logs.

Hiking with children is good exercise as well as an opportunity for learning. Use the time to teach children how to read a compass, identify flowers, trees, birds, and animal tracks. You'll find books on each of these subjects in the public library.

Make it fun by taking a different type of gorp for each hike. Gorp is any combination of dried foods that you eat as a snack. Examples are:
1) peanuts, M&M's®, and raisins
2) chocolate morsels, nuts, and granola
3) dried banana chips, sunflower seeds, and carob chips

Get creative and mix any combination of chocolate, carob, dried fruits, nuts, oats, granolas, etc. The bulk food section at your local grocery store is a wealth of ideas. Other fun snacks are marshmallows, popcorn, peanuts in shells, graham crackers, and beef jerky.

When hiking with a child, tie a string on a whistle and have your child wear it as a necklace for safety. Instruct your child to blow the whistle only if he or she is lost.

Dogs Welcome!

Hiking with dogs can be fun because of their keen sense of smell and different perspective on the world. Many times they find things that we would have passed by. They're inquisitive about everything and make excellent companions. But to ensure that your hiking companion enjoys the time outside, you must control your dog. Dogs are required to be leashed on most maintained public trails. The reasons are numerous, but the top ones are to protect dogs, to protect other hikers, and to ensure your pet doesn't chase wildlife. Good dog manners go a long way toward creating goodwill and improving tolerance toward their presence.

50 of the trails listed in this book welcome dogs. Please respect the requirement that dogs be leashed where noted.

The only trails which **prohibit** dogs are:

Trail #	Trail Name
1	Braddock Bay Raptor Research Trail
10	Genesee Country Nature Center
13	Tinker Nature Park
18	Birdsong Trail (Mendon Ponds Park)
19	Quaker Pond Trail (Mendon Ponds Park
21	Mendon Grasslands Trail (Mendon Ponds Park)
27	Bluebird Haven Trail
43	Thousand Acre Swamp
52	Helmer Nature Center
57	Rochester City Skyway

Seasons

Most people head into the great outdoors in summer. Temperatures are warm, the days are long, and plants and wildlife are plentiful. Summer is a great time to go hiking. But don't neglect the other seasons. Each season offers a unique perspective, and makes hiking the same trail a totally different adventure. In spring, a time of rebirth, you can watch the leaves unfurl and the spring flowers burst.

Become a leaf peeper in fall. Venture forth onto the trails and take in the colorful splendor of a beautiful fall day. Listen to the rustle of newly fallen leaves under your feet and inhale the unique smell of this glorious season.

The only complication with fall is that it coincides with hunting season. The vast majority of trails in this book are in parks or suburban areas where hunting is not permitted. The only exceptions might be Quinn Oak Openings and Genesee Valley Greenway. Wear blaze orange when hiking in the fall on land that may be used for hunting.

And, finally, winter. It may be cold out, but the leaves are off the trees and the views will never be better. You can more fully appreciate the variety of this area's terrain if you wander out in winter. It is also the perfect time to watch for animal tracks in the snow and test your identification skills.

Northwest
Section

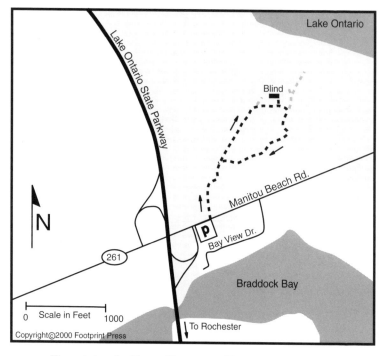

Braddock Bay Raptor Research Trail

1.
Braddock Bay Raptor Research Trail

Location:	Manitou Beach Road, Hilton
Directions:	From Lake Ontario State Parkway, exit at Manitou Beach Road. The parking area is on the northeast side of the exit ramp.

Alternate Parking: None
Hiking Time: 45 minutes
Length: 0.9 mile loop
Difficulty: 🥾🥾

Surface:	Woodchip path and boardwalks
Trail Markings:	None
Uses:	🚶
Dogs:	Pets are NOT allowed
Admission:	Free
Contact:	Braddock Bay Raptor Research 432 Manitou Beach Road Hilton, NY 14468
	N.Y.S. D.E.C. Regional Office 6274 Avon-Lima Road Avon, NY 14414 (716) 226-2466

Visit Braddock Bay Raptor Research Trail in the spring to get a close look at owls and hawks as they migrate north. Upwards of 100,000 hawks, eagles, falcons, and vultures migrate over Braddock Bay along Lake Ontario each spring. The birds find it difficult to fly over the cold waters of Lake Ontario and prefer to fly around it. Braddock Bay is located on a point where the shoreline dips south. Because of the dip, birds stop to rest and get concentrated in this area during migration.

This migration of raptors or "birds of prey" offers a unique opportunity to learn a great deal about the birds. One common research technique is capturing, banding, and releasing the birds.

A hawk-banding blind was built in 1984 and is open for visitation. This is the only banding station in North America with an open door policy. However, you must adhere to the following guidelines, or the policy could change.

21

Policy Guidelines for the Hawk-Banding Area

- Enter only by the back door via the boardwalk from the main trail.
- When you can see the back of the blind, yell "Clear?" and wait for a response. If there is no answer, wait where you are. No response could mean the operators haven't heard you or they are remaining quiet because a hawk is nearby. Try calling again after 30 seconds. If the response is "No," wait until the operator gives you clearance to come in.
- If no one answers please do not enter the area or touch the nets and traps. Do not go out to the traps without permission.
- Ask permission to photograph or videotape any bird or trap.
- Sometimes the blind can become crowded, and the operator will request either that you take only a short look or that you come back at a later time.

From March through May hawks migrate during the day. Owls migrate at night, sleeping in the pine forest and thickets till evening, when they continue their journey. The trail wraps around and through this small grouping of pine trees allowing the opportunity to view the birds up close if you're lucky. The most common species of owls you will see is the northern saw-whet, but others such as the long-eared, short-eared, and great-horned have been seen here also. Informative signs along the trail teach about the

James Miles and Michael Peter enjoy bird watching along
Braddock Bay Raptor Research Trail.

migrating owls and the habitat they prefer. Remember, this area was established to help protect raptors. We are the visitors and should be respectful by being quiet and staying on the established trails.

Also, nearby Braddock Bay Park has a hawk-watch platform for bird spotting. During the spring many people volunteer to count the various species flying high over the Rochester skies. Don't forget to bring your binoculars.

Trail Directions
- From the parking area head north across Manitou Beach Road.
- Follow the mulched trail past scrub brush.
- Cross a boardwalk and continue straight on the trail.
- Continue straight (NE) past a trail to the right and a sign "To Hawk Blind BBRR."
- Cross a small wooden bridge.
- Three trails lead from the left into the bird-banding field. Please take the middle one to visit the blind. It has a boardwalk entrance.
- After visiting the blind, return to the main trail and turn left.
- At 0.4 mile reach a "T." Turn right (S).
- The trail bends right and takes you over a series of boardwalks. (The pine woods on the left is a favorite owl resting area.)
- At 0.8 mile, turn left at the trail junction to return to the parking area.

Date Hiked: _____

Notes:

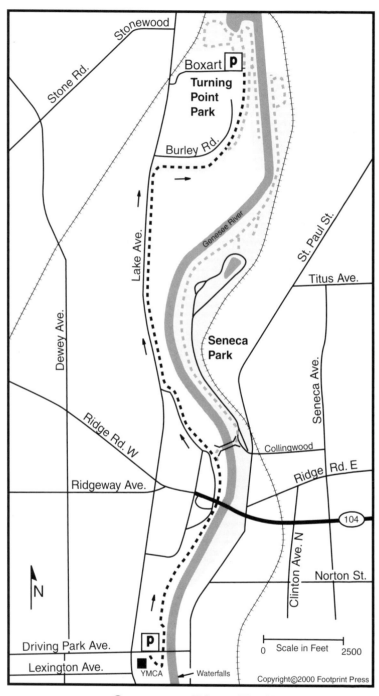

Genesee River Trail

2.
Genesee River Trail

Location:	City of Rochester, from Maplewood Park to Turning Point Park
Directions:	Park in the Maplewood Park parking area on Driving Park Avenue, near the Genesee River.
Alternative Parking:	From Lake Avenue in Charlotte, turn east on Boxart Street. The parking area for Turning Point Park is at the end of Boxart Street.
Hiking Time:	3.5 hours
Length:	7 miles round trip
Difficulty:	🥾 🥾
Surface:	Paved path, mowed grass path, dirt path, and sidewalks
Trail Markings:	Large "Genesee River Trail" signs
Uses:	🚶 🎿
Dogs:	OK on leash
Admission:	Free
Contact:	City of Rochester Bureau of Parks & Recreation
	400 Dewey Avenue
	Rochester, NY 14613
	(716) 428-6770

This linear trail is inside the city limits of Rochester and offers good views of the Genesee River from high above to up close. It begins at the south end of Maplewood Park and ends in Turning Point Park. Along the way you'll get a view of the Genesee River lower falls, cross under the Driving Park and Memorial Bridges, and pass historic King's Landing.

History abounds along this area of the gorge. The early settlements of McCrackenville, Carthage, King's Landing, Frankfort, and Castleton are all but memories. Only Charlotte remains a familiar name. With the coming of the Erie Canal, Rochesterville grew. By 1834 the combination of these seven settlements became the city of Rochester.

The parks at either end of this hike are unique public lands. First, manicured Maplewood Park with its rolling hills, perched next to the Genesee River gorge, is home to 14 acres of rose gardens. Next, Turning Point Park covers 100 acres off Lake Avenue at Boxart Street. This forever-wild park, which sits along the west side of the Genesee River, has docks jutting into the river. A visit will step you back to what Rochester may have looked like 150 years ago. You'll pass old piers where ships tied up. The original docks opened in the 1890s, but only a cement ship comes up the river to deliver its cargo now. This area is the wide-water section of the river where large boats turned around after unloading their cargo. That's how the Turning Point Park got its name. In 1982, a 100-foot long dock was added as a park improvement project.

A winter view of Driving Park Bridge from the Genesee River Trail.

Trail Directions
- Begin by walking across Driving Park Avenue toward the YMCA. On the left side of the YMCA parking lot (west side of Driving Park bridge) is a metal gate.
- Pass by the gate and head down the paved walkway. (Ignore the warning signs. You will not be going near water level where the danger exists.)
- Part way down, take the stairway on the left and double back along the river. (Straight will take you to Rochester Gas and Electric property.) You're rewarded with a great view of Lower Genesee Falls and the Driving Park Bridge.
- At 0.2 mile, pass under Driving Park Bridge.
- Just before heading up a flight of stairs, notice the ruins of an old building ahead near the edge of the gorge. This is the foundation for a refreshment stand built in the early 1900s.

- Climb two flights of stairs to return to Maplewood Park. Be sure to read the historic signs about the underground railroad and the Seneca Indian village. Also directly ahead is a popular winter sledding hill. Children of all ages start at the top next to Lake Avenue and slide toward the Maplewood Park parking lot.
- At 0.3 mile, turn right and follow the fence line as it parallels the river. Genesee River Trail signs will guide you.
- Pass several scenic overlooks with great views of the river gorge.
- Pass under the Veterans Bridge (Route 104).
- Continue following the fence line. Eventually a right turn would take you to a pedestrian bridge over the river to Seneca Park, but that's a separate hike, so continue straight. (See Olmsted/Seneca Trail #51, page 202)
- You'll pass more history: a sign about a palisaded fort of the Indians and a grist stone from Hanford's Mill. Continue along the fence line.
- Pass Eastman Kodak Company's King's Landing Wastewater Treatment plant entrance. Just beyond is a bench with a great view of the river gorge.
- From the bench on you'll be walking approximately 1.5 miles on the sidewalk. Turn right on Lake Avenue and continue on the sidewalk.
- Pass the Kodak research laboratories, Holy Sepulchre Cemetery, and Riverside Cemetery.
- After the cemeteries (just before the Charlotte sign), turn right into Turning Point Park.
- Head downhill on a paved path.
- At the first junction continue straight on the paved path. (The trail to the right is part of the Turning Point Park Trail #53, page 209.)
- Continue downhill to the Turning Point Park parking lot and another great view of the river below.

Date Hiked: _____

Notes:

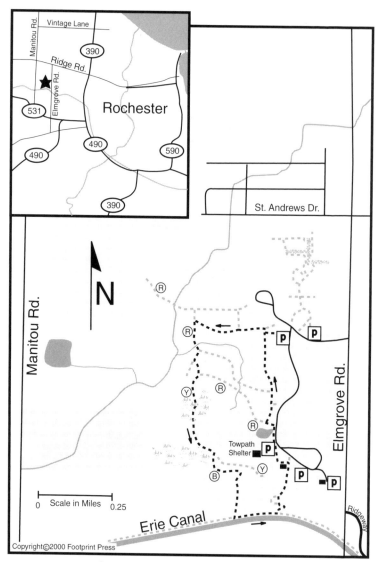

Greece Canal Park Trail

3.
Greece Canal Park Trail

Location: Greece Canal Park, Greece
Directions: From Ridge Road West, turn south on Elmgrove Road.
                     Turn west into Greece Canal Park. Take the first left
                     and park immediately on the right.
Alternate Parking: Towpath Shelter parking area
Hiking Time: 75 minutes
Length: 2.2 mile loop
Difficulty: 👣 👣
                     👣 👣

Surface: Dirt trail
Trail Markings: Red and yellow blazes and 4-inch round plastic yellow
                     markers
Uses: 🚶

Dogs: OK on leash
Admission: Free
Contact: Monroe County Parks Department
                     171 Reservoir Avenue, Rochester, NY 14620

This loop takes you through woods and wetlands and includes a 0.2 mile walk along the Erie Canal. It can be muddy in wet weather. Watch for poison ivy along the trail.

Trail Directions
- From the parking area head northwest on the trail.
- Reach a "T" at 0.1 mile. Turn right (NE).
- Quickly climb a small rise to another "T." Turn left (W).
- Continue straight (NW) past a trail to the right.
- At 0.3 mile, reach a "T" with the red-blazed trail. Turn left (SW).
- Cross a stream on a bridge at 0.4 mile.
- Continue straight (S) on the red-blazed trail, passing a small trail to the left.
- At 0.5 mile, turn left to stay on the red trail. (Straight leads to an airfield on private property.)
- Cross a log bridge over a wet area.
- At 0.7 mile, reach a "T," turn right (W) onto a yellow-blazed trail.
- Cross a small log bridge.

- Reach a junction at 1.0 mile, bear right on the blue-blazed trail. (The yellow-blazed trail to the left leads to a mowed grass area near Towpath Shelter.)
- Cross corduroy as you continue straight through a field.
- At 1.2 miles, climb the bank to the Erie Canal. Turn left (E) and follow the Erie Canalway Trail along the canal.
- At 1.4 miles reach a "Greece Canal Park" sign and a dock. Turn left (N) and head downhill on a paved path.
- Continue downhill on stairs.
- Pass restrooms then turn left on a paved path.
- Cross through the Towpath Shelter parking area. Follow the grass area along the main road, heading north.
- Pass a pond on your left.
- Just after the pond (at 1.7 miles) turn left at the red blaze and enter the woods.
- Watch for the red-blazed trail to turn left. (Straight leads to well-trodden trails through a small quarry area.)
- Immediately after the small, dry quarry, turn right (N) so the quarry is now to your right.
- Stay on the wide path, heading north.
- At 1.9 miles, pass a trail to the left. Continue straight (N).
- At 2.1 miles, turn right (W) and head back to the parking area.

Date Hiked: _____
Notes:

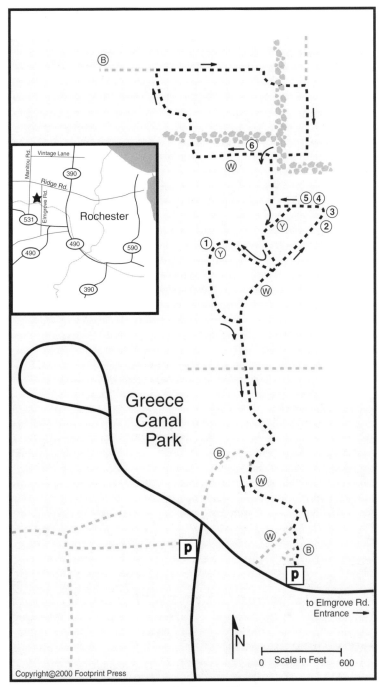

Farm Artifact Trail

4.
Farm Artifact Trail

Location:	Greece Canal Park, Greece
Directions:	From Ridge Road West, turn south on Elmgrove Road. Turn west into Greece Canal Park. The parking area is immediately on the right.

Alternate Parking: None
Hiking Time: 35 minutes
Length: 1.1 mile loop
Difficulty: 🥾

Surface: Woodchip and dirt paths
Trail Markings: White, blue, and yellow blazes
Uses: 🚶

Dogs: OK on leash
Admission: Free
Contact: Monroe County Parks Department
171 Reservoir Avenue, Rochester, NY 14620

As you walk this trail, think back to the days when farmers worked the soil to produce crops. There are stone walls in many places along the way that were used to separate fields. Where do you think the stones came from? Your vision will be assisted by farm artifacts left on the land when farming ceased. This is a treasure hunt trail. See if you can find all 6 farm artifacts:

1. Plow — This double-bottom plow could be pulled by a horse or a tractor. The two blades would each turn the earth to one side, making furrows. Why do you think each wheel is on a separate axle?

2. Drag — The drag loosens the earth and pulls up small stones. The handle could adjust how deep the curved piece would go. Would a farmer use the drag before or after the plow?

3. Hay Rake — This rakes hay into piles for making bales. Some pieces are missing. What do you think the missing pieces looked like?

4. Wagon — The wooden parts of this wagon rotted away. The metal axis and curved parts for steering were left. How long do you think it would take for the wooden parts to rot?

5. Wheel — Envision a bumpy ride in the hay wagon on this metal wheel.

6. Windmill Blades — Windmills catch the energy of the wind and make it do useful work. Windmills were used to pump water, grind grain into flour, and even run sawmills. What do you think the farmer used this windmill for?

You will be following the blue and white-blazed trail north and use the yellow-blazed side loops on your return journey. Beware of poison ivy along the edges of the trail.

Windmill blades.
One of several artifacts found along the Farm Artifact Trail.

Trail Directions

- From the parking area head north on the blue-blazed trail.
- Continue straight past a small blue-blazed loop to the left. The trail snakes through the woods.
- Pass a white-blazed trail to the left. It's a cut-off trail that is blocked off.
- Reach a "T," and turn right (NE) onto the white trail.
- At 0.2 mile, bear right (N) on the white trail. (Straight is the blue-blazed trail.)
- Continue straight, crossing a wide mowed-grass path. (Right goes to private land. Left leads to a sports field.)
- Shortly, pass a yellow trail to the left. Bear right staying on white.
- Pass two other yellow trails on the left at 0.3 mile. Bear right to stay on white.
- Notice the first of the stone walls. Watch for artifacts 2,3,4, and 5 as you walk beside the walls.
- At 0.4 mile, pass another yellow trail to the left. Continue straight on white.
- At the "T," turn left. Watch for artifact 6.
- At 0.5 mile, the trail bends sharply right and crosses the stone wall.
- Reach a "T" at 0.6 mile. Turn right (E). Left is a short blue trail to a grass area.)
- Reach a "T" at 0.7 mile, and turn right (S).
- At the next intersection turn left (S) onto the white-blazed trail.
- Turn right (S) onto the yellow-blazed trail.
- At a "T" turn right on a white trail then an immediate right onto yellow.
- Pass the windmill (artifact 1) at 0.8 mile.
- Reach a white "T" and turn right.
- Cross the wide grass path.
- At 0.9 mile, turn left to stay on the white-blazed trail. (The blue trail to the left leads to the park road.)
- Turn left onto the blue trail. (Straight ahead the white trail leads to the road.)
- Follow the blue trail as it winds back to the parking area.

Date Hiked: _____

Notes:

Northampton Park

This 973 acre park is unique because of the active "working" farm within its boundaries. Originally, when the park was dedicated in 1964, it was named Salmon Creek Park. But, Northampton was later selected to honor the area's rich history and the former Township of Northampton.

The park, which straddles the Sweden-Ogden town line, combines a downhill ski slope and rope tow, a model airplane field, Salmon Creek, the Pulver House of the Ogden Historical Society, and Springdale Farm — a demonstration farm with chickens, peacocks, turkeys, horses, cows, goats, bunnies, pigs, lambs, and bulls. It's a great place to explore with children either before or after a hike. The farm is open Monday through Saturday from 10 AM to 4 PM and Sundays, noon to 4 PM.

Geese paddle along on the Springdale Farm pond.

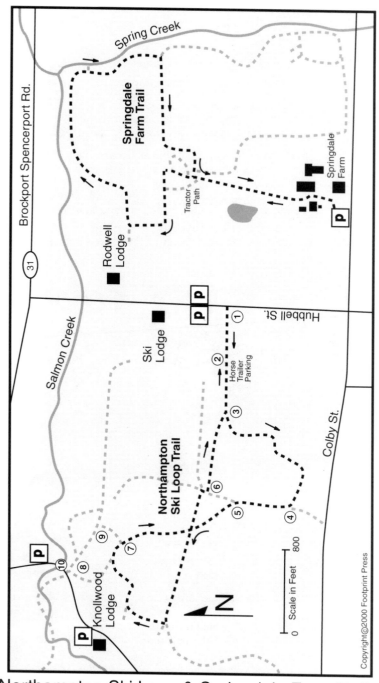

Northampton Ski Loop & Springdale Farm Trails

5.
Springdale Farm Trail

Location:	Northampton Park, Colby Street, Ogden
Directions:	Take Route 31 west from Rochester. Turn south on Route 36 then west on Colby Street. Park in the Springdale Farm parking area.

Alternative Parking: None
Hiking Time: 45 minutes
Length: 1.7 mile loop
Difficulty:

Surface:	Gravel, mulch, dirt, and mowed-grass paths
Trail Markings:	None
Uses:	
Dogs:	OK on leash
Admission:	Free
Contact:	Monroe County Parks Department 171 Reservoir Avenue Rochester, NY 14620 (716) 256-4950
	Springdale Farm operated by Heritage Christian Home, Inc. (716) 352-5320

On this easy-to-walk loop you'll pass the barns and animal pens of Springdale Farm then pass a pond which is home to geese and ducks. A swing, picnic tables and benches make this a restful place to stop before or after your hike. The trail then leads through a forest, skirts the edge of a farm field and enters another forest. You'll walk high on a ledge overlooking Spring Creek then follow the edge of farm fields back to the pond and barn area.

Trail Directions
- From the parking area follow the paved path past Springdale Farms barn area.
- The gravel road leads from behind the barns and past a pond.
- At the "Woodlot Trail" sign, the trail turns to mulch and enters the woods.

- Bear left (NE) at the big red sign and follow the mulched path through a beech tree forest.
- Pass two trails to the right. (They lead to a classroom area and loop back to the big red sign.)
- At 0.4 mile, emerge to a farm field. Turn left (W) and follow the edge of the field.
- Pass a grass trail on the left.
- At the bottom of the sled hill (before heading uphill) turn right (N) and cross the edge of the field.
- Bear right again (E) and follow along the edge of the woods. You're now on the opposite side of the field from where you started.
- At 0.6 mile, enter the woods.
- At 0.9 mile, climb a small hill. Spring Creek is in a gully to your left as you walk through a mature pine forest.
- Pass through a shrub field.
- At 1.1 miles, reach a junction and turn right (W). (Left is a loop that leads toward Colby Street.)
- Follow the edge of a farm field. The trail bends several times. Keep the farm fields to your left.
- Pass a small mowed path to the left. (This leads toward Colby Street and loops back around the farm fields.)
- At 1.4 miles, meet the gravel path. Turn left (SW) and head toward the barns and parking area.

Date Hiked: _____

Notes:

6.
Northampton Ski Loop Trail

Location:	Northampton Park, Hubbell Street, Ogden
Directions:	Take Route 31 west from Rochester. After passing Route 36, turn south on Hubbell Street. Park on the west side of Hubbell Street in the southernmost section of the Ski Lodge parking area.

Alternative Parking: On the east side of Hubbell Street

Hiking Time:	1 hour
Length:	2.0 mile loop (see map on page 36)
Difficulty:	
Surface:	Mowed-grass path
Trail Markings:	Blue-and-white metal signs on wooden posts at some trail junctions
Uses:	
Dogs:	OK on leash
Admission:	Free
Contact:	Monroe County Parks Department 171 Reservoir Avenue Rochester, NY 14620 (716) 256-4950

The vegetation along the trail is mostly tall bush and young trees. It's the perfect habitat for birds. While hiking, you'll be serenaded by the honk of pheasants and the trill of songbirds. In late summer you can pick berries from bushes along the 10-foot wide mowed-grass trail. In winter, glide easily along on skis.

Trail Directions
- Leave the parking area from the corner farthest from the ski lodge, heading southwest through a grove of young pines.
- Cross the grass to to a sign "Horse Trailer Parking" and junction marker #2.
- Continue straight (W) on the mowed-grass path.
- Turn left (S) at junction marker #3.
- The path goes between woods and a field. At 0.5 mile, reach junction marker #4 and turn right (N).

- Notice the old stone wall inside the woods along the right side of the trail — a sure sign that this was once farm land. Farmers cleared stones from their fields and piled them along property lines.
- At junction marker #5 bear left (N).
- After the wide mowed area, turn left. You're now heading west.
- When the path curves at 0.9 mile, bear right. (Two paths lead off to the left.)
- The path is gravel covered for a short stretch.
- Bear right again past a trail to the left. You're now heading east.
- The trail bends several times.
- At 1.2 miles bear right (E) past a trail to the left.
- At junction marker #7 turn right (S).
- At the wide mowed-grass area turn left (E).
- Reach an intersection at 1.5 miles and turn right (S).
- Quickly reach junction marker #6 and turn left (S).
- Cross a short gravel stretch then the trail turns to dirt as you walk through the woods.
- At 1.7 miles, turn left (E) at junction marker #3, and return to the parking area.

Date Hiked: _____
Notes:

Southwest Section

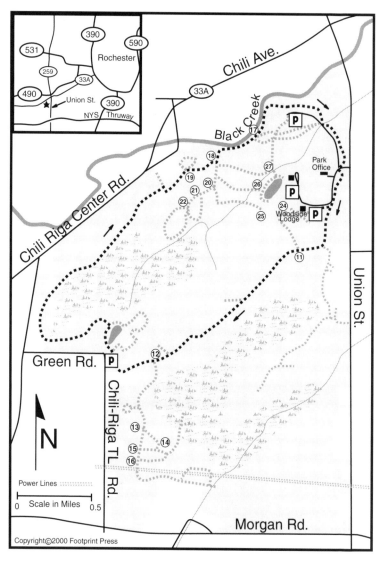

Black Creek Trail

7.
Black Creek Trail

Location: Black Creek Park, Union Street, Chili

Directions: Take the Union Street exit off Interstate 490 and head south on Union Street. Turn right to enter Black Creek Park and follow the park road left to the parking area near Woodside Lodge.

Alternative Parking: At the north end of the park road

Hiking Time: 2 hours and 15 minutes

Length: 4.2 mile loop

Difficulty: 👣 👣

Surface: Mowed-grass and dirt paths

Trail Markings: Some junctions are marked with blue-and-white numbered signs on wooden posts

Uses: 🚶 🎿 🐎

Dogs: OK on leash

Admission: Free

Contact: Monroe County Parks Department
171 Reservoir Avenue, Rochester, NY 14620
(716) 256-4950

Black Creek is the centerpiece of this park in southwestern Monroe County. Purchased in 1963, the park has large tracts of undeveloped, rolling hills with two small ponds. Its trails wind through tall brush and young forest areas which attract many kinds of birds. Six-foot wide paths are mowed throughout the park creating many possible hiking or cross-country skiing loops. Deer are plentiful in the park.

Trail Directions
- From the southeast corner of the parking area, walk east along the mulched trail.
- Turn right (S) and pass a gate.
- Turn right at the "T."
- At 0.2 mile, pass benches on the right overlooking a depression area.
- Pass junction marker #11 and a small trail into the woods on the right. Continue straight (SW).
- At 1.0 mile, enter the woods. Bear left to stay on the main trail.
- Stay on the main trail, passing a small trail to the right.

43

- Reach junction marker #12 at 1.2 miles. Continue straight (W).
- Cross a wooden bridge.
- Bear right toward the red barn.
- At 1.5 miles cross the parking area.
- Bear left around the far side of the pond.
- Half way down the pond, turn left (W) and head uphill into the woods.
- Follow the top of an open ridge then descend into woods.
- At 2.1 miles, cross a small boardwalk then proceed through a wet area.
- Cross a makeshift bridge then a small boardwalk over a creek.
- Reach a mowed area.
- Reach a "T" at 2.3 miles. Turn right (NE). (Left leads to a road.)
- Bear right staying on the wide path when a small trail heads left.
- At 3.1 miles, reach a "T." Turn right (S). (Left leads to Chili Riga Center Road.)
- Continue straight past a trail to the left.
- Turn right to cross a small wooden bridge to junction marker #19.
- At junction marker #18 turn left (NE).
- The trail bends right and Black Creek gully comes into view on the left.
- Pass a trail to the right.
- Reach junction marker #17 with another trail to the right at 3.5 miles.
- Walk through a grassy picnic area.
- At the end of the mowed area, follow the gravel trail uphill.
- Continue straight.
- At 3.7 miles, just before the park road, turn left (SE) on a grass path.
- At 3.9 miles reach a park road. Turn left along the road, then bear left (SE) onto the grass path.
- Continue straight across a park road.
- Follow the grass path back to the parking area.

Date Hiked: _____

Notes:

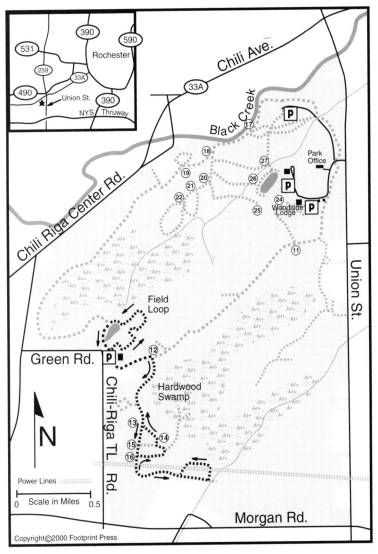

Hardwood Swamp Trail &
Black Creek Field Loop

8.
Hardwood Swamp Trail

Location:	Black Creek Park, Chili-Riga Town Line Road, Chili
Directions:	Take the Union Street exit off Interstate 490 and head south on Union Street. Turn west on Morgan Road, then north on Chili-Riga Town Line Road. The parking area is at the corner of Green Road and Chili-Riga Town Line Road

Alternative Parking: None
Hiking Time: 75 minutes
Length: 2.5 mile loop
Difficulty: 🥾🥾 🥾🥾

Surface:	Mowed-grass path
Trail Markings:	Junctions are marked with blue-and-white numbered signs on wooden posts
Uses:	🚶 🎿 🐎
Dogs:	OK on leash
Admission:	Free
Contact:	Monroe County Parks Department
	171 Reservoir Avenue, Rochester, NY 14620
	(716) 256-4950

This trail is found in the less-used section of Black Creek Park. The wide mowed paths are perfect for a quiet stroll to enjoy sunshine and the sounds of nature. Much of the trail passes through scrub brush fields which a variety of birds call home.

Trail Directions
- From the parking area, bear right (S) past the red barn. At a wide grassy area turn left to find the beginning of the trail.
- Cross the bridge over a small creek.
- At 0.2 mile, reach junction marker #12. Turn right (S).
- Pass a narrow mowed path to the right at 0.4 mile. (This is a 0.3 mile loop.)
- Junction marker #13 is a "Y." Bear right for a gradual uphill walk.
- At 0.6 mile, turn right (S) at junction marker #15.
- Go straight (S) at junction marker #16.
- At 0.8 mile, pass under power lines.

- Cross a low area which may have a running stream in wet times of the year.
- The trail bends east to run along the park property line, parallel to the power lines.
- Pass under the power lines again at 1.0 mile.
- At the "Y," bear right and start uphill, remaining under the power lines.
- After a downhill, you'll see a gravel area with an old bridge over a creek straight ahead. This is a dead end. (Future plans indicate it will continue.) Turn left (NE) and loop back under the power lines.
- The trail meanders up and down hills, wanders left and right, and passes back under the power lines.
- Go straight (W) at the next junction and you are back on the trail you came in on.
- At 1.5 miles, cross the potentially wet lowland again as you pass under the power lines.
- At junction marker #16 turn right (E).
- At 1.8 miles, pass a trail to the right. Continue straight (N). (The side trail dead-ends in 0.3 mile and is loaded with poison ivy.)
- Turn right (N) at junction marker #14.
- At 2.0 miles, continue straight (N) through junction marker #13.
- Pass the small loop trail to the left at 2.1 miles.
- Reach junction marker #12 at 2.2 miles. Turn left (NW).
- Cross the small wooden bridge then turn right to return to the parking area.

Date Hiked: _____

Notes:

9.
Black Creek Field Loop

Location:	Black Creek Park, Chili-Riga Town Line Road, Chili
Directions:	Take the Union Street exit off Interstate 490 and head south on Union Street. Turn west on Morgan Road, then north on Chili-Riga Town Line Road. The parking area is at the corner of Green Road and Chili-Riga Town Line Road

Alternative Parking: None
Hiking Time: 25 minutes
Length: 0.8 mile loop
Difficulty:

Surface: Mowed-grass path
Trail Markings: None
Uses:

Dogs: OK on leash
Admission: Free
Contact: Monroe County Parks Department
171 Reservoir Avenue, Rochester, NY 14620
(716) 256-4950

If you would like a quick introduction to Black Creek Park, try this easy loop around a field and pond on a wide mowed-grass path.

Trail Directions
- From the far end (NW corner) of the parking area, turn left and cross the grassy area (red barn on your right). A man-made pond is visible to your left.
- Follow the mowed path to the right (E) heading away from the pond. The forest is on your right and a field on your left.
- The mowed path takes you around the perimeter of the field, always with woods to your right.
- At 0.6 mile the pond will come into view. Bear right (NW) and cross the grass-covered dike.
- Bear left to keep the pond on your left. (Uphill, across the wide mowed-grass area is the entrance into the woods of the Black Creek Trail, see page 43.)

- At the south end of the pond, walk uphill to the parking area.

Date Hiked: _____

Notes:

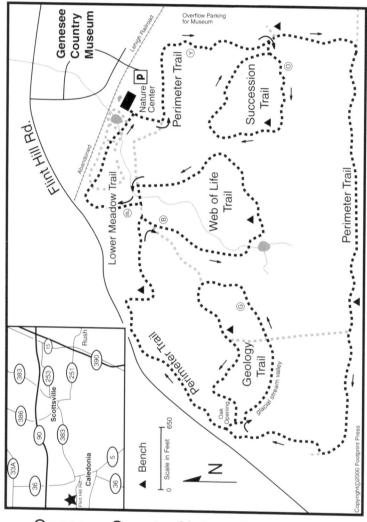

Genesee Country Nature Center Trails

10.
Genesee Country Nature Center Trails

Location:	Genesee Country Museum, Mumford
Directions:	From Route 36, turn west onto Flint Hill Road just north of Caledonia. Turn left into Genesee Country Museum and follow the signs to the nature center parking area.

Alternative Parking: None

Hiking Time:	2 hours (or more if you read the interpretive signs)
Length:	3.5 mile loop
Difficulty:	
Surface:	Mowed-grass, mulched, and dirt paths
Trail Markings:	Wooden trail signs at junctions
Uses:	🚶 🎿
Dogs:	Pets are NOT allowed
Admission:	Adults $2.50, Seniors $2.00, Children 4-16 $1.50, Children under 4 free. Free with admission to Genesee Country Museum
Contact:	Genesee Country Nature Center Flint Hill Road, Mumford, NY 14511 (716) 538-6822 http://www.gcv.org

Genesee Country Museum is a reconstructed community from the 1800s with 57 restored and fully furnished buildings. Stroll the streets and visit each shop, home, school, and church as costumed villagers demonstrate life from a bygone century.

Genesee Country Nature Center is part of Genesee Country Museum. The nature center has a classroom building with nature exhibits, a lily pond, a butterfly garden, and nearly five miles of hiking and cross-country skiing trails. Special events such as guided hikes, birds of prey day, nesting bird surveys, and programs on area wildlife and history are held throughout the year.

Admission to the museum includes admission to the nature center. Or, you can purchase nature center admission separately. In the summer the nature center is open weekdays 10 AM to 4 PM, weekends and holidays, 10

AM to 5 PM. It is closed Mondays. Call (716) 538-6822 for up to date information on admission fees and hours of operation.

The trails within Genesee Country Nature Center are mostly flat with a few rolling hills. The land was once farmed and now contains a mixture of fields and young forest. We particularly enjoyed the interpretive signs along these trails. On the Succession Trail, they teach the process of succession from farm field back to forest. Trees are labeled on the Perimeter Trail. A vernal (or seasonal) pond is the highlight of the Web of Life Trail. It's the breeding site of spotted and blue-spotted salamanders.

The Geology Trail teaches the unique geology of this area, pointing out ancient waterfalls from glacial streams, marine fossils, and oak openings. Approximately 4,000 years ago a major drought caused the demise of many native species of trees and allowed midwestern prairie plants to move east. It created fields of tall grass prairies surrounded by oak forests — an oak opening. The Indians noticed that these grass openings were havens from bugs and allowed them to get a broader view of approaching enemies so they kept the grasslands open with fire. The absence of trees in the oak

Interpretive signs like this one identifying an old stone wall, help the walker learn about geology and history along the nature trails.

openings made them easy targets for farmers. As white settlers moved in, many of the oak openings were put to use to raise crops.

This oak opening is one of fewer than 20 oak openings remaining in the world. It was spared because limestone is only a few inches below the surface so it was hard to plow and virtually impossible to sink fence posts. The other area oak opening can be found at Quinn Oak Openings in Rush. (see trail #12, page 59.)

The loop described here samples each of the trails, giving you a broad look at this special landscape. There are many opportunities to shorten your hike. If you want to do a shorter hike, the loop distances from the nature center are as follows:

Perimeter Trail (yellow)	1.9 miles
Geology Trail (green)	1.8 miles
Succession Trail (orange)	1.1 miles
Web of Life Trail (blue)	0.8 mile
Lower Meadow Trail (black)	0.3 mile

The nature center personnel told us that the Web of Life Trail was the most heavily used. We could see that by its well worn path. But, by far, our favorite trail was the Geology Trail because of it's unusual geologic characteristics and the excellent signs along the way that helped us understand the land we stood upon.

Trail Directions

- Head out the back door of the nature center building.
- Bear left (S) on the yellow Perimeter Trail.
- Turn left (S) at the "T" to stay on the Perimeter Trail.
- At 0.3 mile, turn right onto the orange Succession Trail.
- Follow the orange arrow, bearing left.
- Reach a junction at 0.8 mile and turn left.
- Quickly reach a "T," and turn right (SE) to return to the Perimeter Trail.
- Bear right. (Left leads to a parking area.)
- At 0.9 mile the trail bends right so you're now walking west in a young forest.
- Reach a bent tree at 1.3 miles and a bench shortly thereafter.
- At 1.4 miles, pass an unmarked trail to the right. Continue straight.
- The trail bends right and begins heading north.
- The trail bends right again. (The trail straight ahead is blocked off.)
- At 1.6 miles, reach a ridge. The trail bends left (NW) to follow the ridge then does a U turn to descend the ridge.
- Turn right (S) at 1.7 miles onto the green Geology Trail.
- Soon bear right (S) to head into the glacial stream valley.
- Pass an extinct waterfall then proceed through a valley formed by glacial floods 14,000 years ago.

- At 1.9 miles, pass an intersection. Continue straight.
- Pass remains of a high stone wall at 2.0 miles.
- Reach a "T," and turn left (W) onto the Geology Trail.
- Pass a bench at 2.1 miles as you walk a ridge.
- Follow the arrow sign, bearing right.
- Head downhill then pass over another old stone wall.
- At 2.3 miles, cross a small wooden bridge.
- Enter the oak savannah (also called an oak opening).
- Continue straight past a trail to the left.
- Reach a "T." Turn right (E).
- At 2.4 miles pass an old well on your right.
- Pass a bench at 2.6 miles, then pass through another old stone wall.
- At 2.8 miles turn right (SW) at the "T" onto the blue Web of Life Trail.
- Bear left.
- Cross a stream culvert. Vernal Pond is to your right.
- Pass a bench at 3.0 miles.
- Head downhill.
- Turn left (W) at the "T" onto The Perimeter Trail.
- Quickly take a right (N) onto The Lower Meadow Trail.
- At 3.4 miles, emerge to the meadow.
- Continue straight passing a series of mowed paths in the meadow to return to the nature center building.

Date Hiked: _____

Notes:

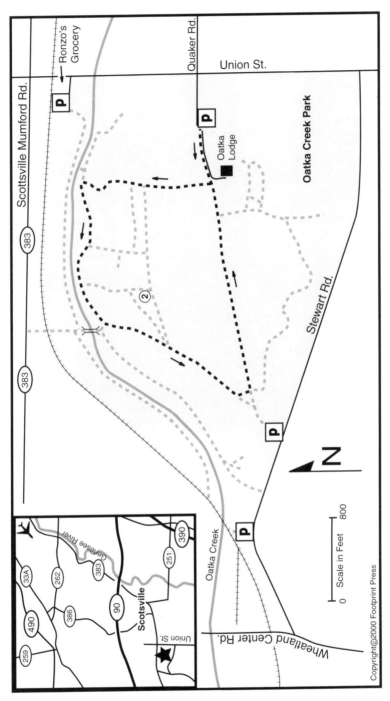

Plaster Woods Trail

11.
Plaster Woods Trail

Location: Oatka Creek Park, Scottsville

Directions: From Scottsville, head west on Route 383 (Scottsville Mumford Road.) Turn south on Union Street and west into the parking area of Oatka Creek Park at the end of Quaker Road.

Alternative Parking: The parking area behind Ronzo's Grocery on Union Street

The pull-off areas on Stewart Road

Hiking Time: 1 hour

Length: 2.0 mile loop

Difficulty: 👣 👣

Surface: Gravel, mowed-grass, and dirt paths

Trail Markings: None

Uses: 🚶 🥾

Dogs: OK on leash

Admission: Free

Contact: Monroe County Parks Department
171 Reservoir Avenue, Rochester, NY 14620
(716) 256-4950

Under this lush, wooded park lies a soft-gray colored rock called gypsum. Gypsum was used by early farmers as fertilizer, later becoming this country's first cement. Today it is used in wallboard for home construction. Chemically, gypsum is calcium sulfate and gradually turns soil sour (or acidic). Because dogwood, azalea, and mosses prefer this type of soil, these types of vegetation abound in Oatka Creek Park.

When the trail nears the south side of Oatka Creek, you will notice many pits and mounds, remnants of where workers dug gypsum by hand over 150 years ago. They hauled it to the surface with ropes, loaded it into small carts, and pulled it by mules to a mill nearby. You may also find old grist

Marcy Fenton, Alex James Clar, and dalmations TJ and Dooley stretch their legs on Plaster Woods Trail.

Fly fishing in Oatka Creek.

mill foundations and signs of an early settler's log cabin. To fully explore the gypsum pits and mounds, wander the trails in the northeast part of the park, south of Oatka Creek.

Oatka Creek Park is best known for brown trout fishing in Oatka Creek. You're likely to see people fly fishing in the creek. And, if you enjoy bird watching, this is the place. Watch for downy woodpeckers, flickers, eastern bluebirds and many others, especially in the scrub brush fields.

Trail Directions

- From the parking area head west on the old gravel road, passing Oatka Lodge on the left.
- Turn right (N) just past the yellow guardrail and gate onto a narrow dirt trail.
- Continue straight as you pass first one trail, then another trail to your left. You'll begin to see gypsum potholes.
- At 0.6 mile, the trail "Ts." Turn left (NW) following a ridge above Oatka Creek.
- At the next intersection bear right.
- Continue straight. A trail comes in from the left.
- Bear left at the next "Y." (Right leads to the creek.)
- At 0.8 mile, reach a wide mowed-grass area with a trail to the left. (This leads south to a junction labeled #2.) Continue straight (NW).
- At the next "Y" junction follow the wide trail to the left (SW). (Trail to the right goes over a concrete bridge to connect with the fishing access trail on the north side of Oatka Creek. It provides a nice view of the creek.)
- Walk up the hill, through a shrub field, to where two trails enter from the left. Bear right (SW).

- Reach a "Y" junction at 1.3 miles and bear left (S).
- This is quickly followed by a four-way intersection. Turn left (E) onto what once was Quaker Road.
- Continue straight (E) past a trail to the right at 1.7 miles.
- Continue straight through an intersection and past Oatka Lodge to return to the parking area.

Bonus:

If you would like to see more of this park and up-close views of Oatka Creek, drive north on Union Street. After crossing the creek look for Ronzo's Grocery on your left, and park in the fisherman's lot behind the store. Follow the path from the southwest corner to the creek. You are able to walk along the creek to the concrete bridge (at 0.6 mile) and beyond before having to turn around as the trail ends at the railroad tracks in 1.3 miles. Walking this additional section takes about 1.25 hours.

Date Hiked: _____
Notes:

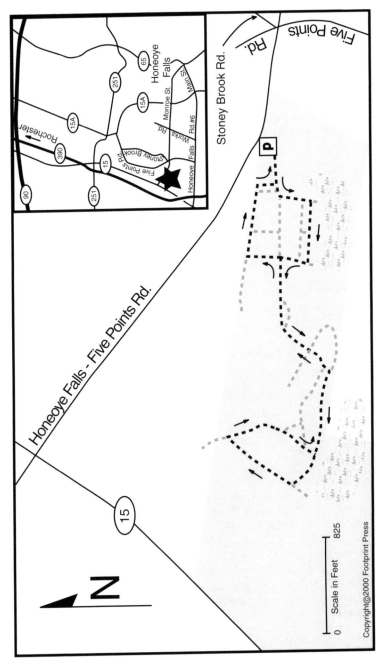

Quinn Oak Openings

12.
Quinn Oak Openings

Location:	Honeoye Falls-Five Points Road, Rush
Directions:	From Route 15 (south of Rochester), turn east on Honeoye Falls-Five Points Road. Watch for the Quinn Oak Openings parking area on the south side of Honeoye Falls-Five Points Road.

Additional Parking: None

Hiking Time: 45 minutes

Length: 1.5 mile loop

Difficulty:

Surface: Dirt and mowed field trails

Trail Markings: None

Uses:

Dogs: OK

Admission: Free

Contact: N.Y.S. Department of Environmental
Conservation – Forestry
7291 Coon Road, Bath, NY 14810
(607) 776-2165 ext. 10
http://www.dec.state.ny.us

The sign at the parking area reads "Quinn Oak Openings – Area of Exceptional Forest Character." We'll vouch for the exceptional character of the forests, grass fields, scrub brush fields, and swamps. This wonderfully diverse area is home to many birds, butterflies, animals, and over 400 species of plants. It's also a magical place for us humans to wander.

Approximately 4,000 years ago a major drought caused the demise of many native species of trees and allowed midwestern prairie plants to move east. It created fields of tall grass prairies surrounded by oak forests – an oak opening. The Indians noticed that these grass openings were havens from bugs and allowed them to get a broader view of approaching enemies so they kept the grasslands open with fire. The absence of trees in the oak openings made them easy targets for farmers. As white settlers moved in, many of the oak openings were put to use to raise crops.

Quinn Oak Openings is one of fewer than 20 oak openings remaining in the world. Like another opening close by (see the Genesee Country Nature Center Trails on page 51), it was spared because limestone is only a few inches below the surface. This land was privately owned and was used to graze cows. The farmers continued periodic burnings to encourage grass growth. Today, D.E.C. continues this practice to save this unique resource.

The trails can be a challenge to follow. They may be overgrown if it's been awhile since the last mowing or obscured by a blanket of leaves in fall. Sometimes the D.E.C. mows new channels through the grasslands, so the trails shown on the map may vary. Even so, this area is worth exploration. It's unlikely that you'll run into other humans. You're much more likely to scare up deer during your walk. Pay attention to the trees along the way. You'll find rare cinquapin oak and prickly ash. The grass is called indian grass and grows 6 to 7 feet tall. It's quite a sight in September at its full height with seed heads waving in the autumn breeze.

Trail Directions
- Pass the blue metal gate as you head west on a wide, mowed-grass path. (You're not likely to notice the trails on the right.)
- Turn left (S) onto the first trail to the left. It will appear as a clearing comes into view.
- Take the second right (W) onto a 20-foot wide, uneven weedy swath. (Heading straight past this turnoff will land you in a swamp.)
- Pass a mowed trail to the right.
- Turn right at the "T," passing mowed strips.
- Cross a mowed-grass area, then turn left (W) onto the main trail at 0.3 mile.
- At the "Y" you have a choice. Go left for high, dry ground or, bear right for level, potentially wet ground. The paths converge in 100 feet.
- Stay on the main trail (two tire tracks) as it bends left.
- Pass an intersecting trail and cross a seasonal creek swale. Continue straight on the main path.
- Enter a young forest. (A small trail enters from the right, but we bet you won't see it.)
- At 0.4 mile, turn right (W) at the "T" junction.
- Continue straight past a trail to the right. (This will be part of the return loop.)
- The trail will become rocky and hilly.
- Turn right (N) at the "T" junction.
- The trail bed returns to dirt and mowed grass.
- Turn right (SW) at the "T" junction to stay on the wide mowed path. (The path to the left dead-ends.)
- Bear right and pass a small trail to the left. (You can walk the small trail loops as shown on the map but they may not be maintained.)
- Pass a second small trail on the left.
- At 0.9 mile, turn left (E) at the "T" junction.

- At the next junction, turn left (NE). (The path bearing right loops through a 0.1-mile swampy area and should only be taken if the trails are dry.)
- Immediately pass a small, barely visible trail on your left.
- Continue past the seasonal stream and another trail junction. (This is where the 0.1-mile swampy loop returns.)
- At the "Y" junction, choose either option. A right will take you over high ground, left will be low ground. The paths converge in a short distance.
- At 1.2 miles, turn left (N) when you see a wide mowed area to your right.
- Turn right (E) at the "T" junction. (The trail to the left meanders through moss-covered rocks in a forest but dead-ends.)
- Pass several small trails to the right.
- The trail will bend sharply right (S) and meet the main trail.
- Turn left (E) onto the main trail for a short distance back to the parking area.

Date Hiked: _____

Notes:

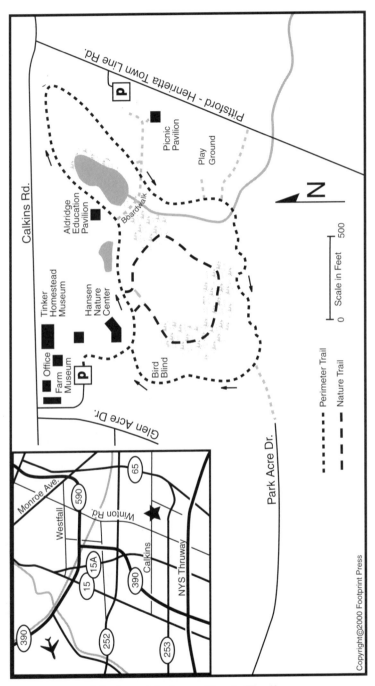

Tinker Nature Park Trails

13.
Tinker Nature Park Trails

Location: Calkins Road, Henrietta

Directions: Tinker Nature Park parking area is at 1525 Calkins Road, Henrietta (between Pinnacle Road and Pittsford-Henrietta Town Line Road).

Alternate Parking: The parking area off Pittsford-Henrietta Town Line Road

Hiking Time: 45 minutes (Perimeter Trail)
20 minutes (Nature Trail)

Length: 1.2 mile loop (Perimeter Trail)
0.5 mile loop (Nature Trail)

Difficulty:

Surface: Gravel path, mulched trails, and boardwalks

Trail Markings: Some wooden signs

Uses:

Dogs: Pets are NOT allowed

Admission: Free

Contact: Tinker Nature Park
1525 Calkins Road, Pittsford, NY 14534
PO Box 999, Henrietta, NY 14467
(716) 359-7044

Tinker Homestead and Farm Museum
1585 Calkins Road, Pittsford, NY 14534-2719
PO Box 999, Henrietta, NY 14467
(716) 359-7042

The land for Tinker Nature Park was donated by the Aldridge family in 1991 and made public in 1994. The well designed park has become a year-round favorite for people of all ages. It consists of woods, wetland, ponds, and fields which together create a living museum of natural history. Within the park is the Hansen Nature Center, offering classes in cross-country skiing, snowshoeing, photography, wild flowers, song birds, etc. The nature center building is open Tuesday through Saturday, 9 AM to 3 PM, and Sundays 11 AM to 3 PM.

While there you will also want to visit the Tinker Homestead built in 1830. This turn of the century cobblestone museum is free and open to the

A perfect day for a stroll at Tinker Nature Park.
Teresa Hirschman is joined by Rebecca, Ryan, and Elizabeth.

public, with guided tours Tuesday through Thursday and Saturdays and Sundays, noon to 4 PM, other times by appointment.

Two trails are available for hiking. Choose one or combine them for a longer hike. The Perimeter Trail has exercise stations along the way. Both trails have abundant wildlife. On a spring hike we saw nesting Canada geese, a big fat raccoon, turtles, ducks, woodpeckers, chipmunks, squirrels, and song birds too numerous to name. We listened to the music of spring peepers (a type of frog) and walked through forests carpeted with May apples.

Trail Directions — Perimeter Trail

- From the parking area follow the brick path.
- Pass the Perimeter Trail on your right. (This will be part of the return loop.)
- Pass the front of the nature center building.
- Pass the Nature Trail on the right.
- Continue on the gravel path. Pass the third trail to the right. (This also leads to the Nature Trail.) A marsh is on your left.

- At 0.2 mile, pass the Boardwalk Trail to the right. (It offers an up-close view of a pond.)
- The trail bends right and eventually heads southwest.
- Pass a trail to the left which leads to the parking area on Pittsford-Henrietta Town Line Road.
- At 0.6 mile, the Boardwalk Trail rejoins the Perimeter Trail from the right.
- A trail to the left leads to a playground area.
- Enter the woods.
- At 0.7 mile, a trail to the left leads to Pittsford-Henrietta Town Line Road. Continue straight and cross a wooden bridge.
- Wind through the woods.
- Cross bridges over a marsh area.
- Reach a junction at 1.0 mile and bear right. (Left leads to Park Acre Drive.) Cross more bridges.
- Emerge to a grass area and a bird blind where you can observe song birds at feeders.
- Follow the split rail fence back to the nature center building.
- At the "T," turn left to return to the parking area. (Or, turn right to continue on the Nature Trail.)

Date Hiked: _____

Notes:

The boardwalk at Tinker Nature Park.

Trail Directions — Nature Trail

- From the parking area follow the brick path.
- Pass the Perimeter Trail on your right.
- Pass the front of the nature center building.
- Turn right onto the Nature Trail.
- At the "Y," bear right.
- Cross a wooden bridge.
- The trail loops left to a boardwalk over the swamp.
- At the "T," turn right.
- Meet a gravel trail and turn left.
- Pass the Nature Trail entrance on the left and the nature center building on the right.
- Bear right to return to the parking area.

Date Hiked: _____
Notes:

Genesee Valley Greenway

The Genesee Valley Greenway is a 90-mile historic and natural resource corridor which follows a transportation route that was used by the Genesee Valley Canal, from 1840 to 1878, and by the railroad, from 1880 to the mid 1960s. The former rail bed now serves as a multi-use trail open to hikers, bikers, horseback riders, cross-country skiers, and snowmobilers. Currently, 47 miles of the total 90 miles are open for use. Each year, more segments are opened.

Two segments are described in this book. The first runs from Genesee Valley Park in Rochester to Route 383, near the airport. The second heads from Scottsville, south to Avon, or north to Route 252. Additional sections south of Avon are described in the book *Take Your Bike! Family Rides in the Finger Lakes and Genesee Valley Region.*

The Genesee Valley Greenway connects with the Rochester River Trail, the Erie Canalway Trail, the Finger Lakes Trail, as well as Rochester's Genesee Valley Park and Letchworth State Park. It will eventually connect to the Lehigh Valley Trail as well.

The Genesee Valley Greenway passes through wetlands, woodlands, rolling farmlands, steep gorges, historic villages, and the Genesee and Black Creek valleys. It offers something for everyone, from a short outing to a challenging long-distance trek. You can stop to explore quaint villages, visit an historic canal era inn, or inspect well-preserved stone locks and other remnants of the ingenuity and engineering that built the canal and the railroad.

This trail is a work-in-progress. Each year more mileage is opened and segments are being connected. The signage along the trail has been significantly improved. When in doubt, follow the posted Genesee Valley Greenway signs to stay on the most recent routing of the trail.

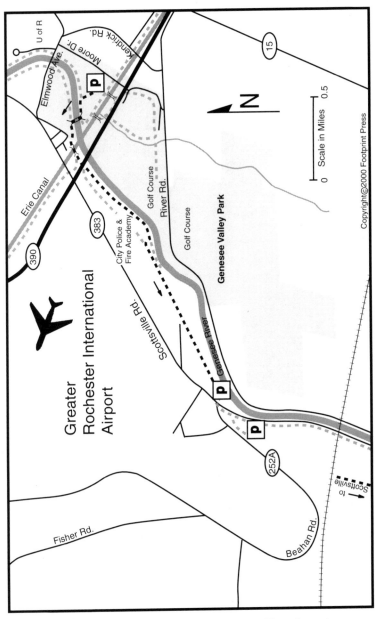

Genesee Valley Greenway - Rochester

14.
Genesee Valley Greenway
Rochester

Location:	Genesee Valley Park to Scottsville Road (Route 383)
Directions:	From Elmwood Avenue near the University of Rochester, turn southwest into Genesee Valley Park on Moore Drive. Park at the Roundhouse Pavilion parking area off Moore Drive.

Alternative Parking: Route 383 near the intersection of Route 252A, next to Gillirmos American Italian Restaurant

Hiking Time: 75 minutes one way

Length: 2.2 miles one way

Difficulty:

Surface: Paved path

Trail Markings: Some directional signs and some "Genesee Valley Greenway" signs

Uses:

Dogs: OK on leash

Admission: Free

Contact: City of Rochester - Bureau of Parks & Recreation
400 Dewey Avenue, Rochester, NY 14613
(716) 428-6770

Friends of the Genesee Valley Greenway, Inc.
P.O. Box 42
Mount Morris, NY 14510
(716) 658-2569
http://www.netacc.net/~fogvg

From Genesee Valley Park where the Erie Canal meets the Genesee River, follow this newly paved, easy-walking trail as it snakes southwest along the Genesee River heading toward Scottsville. Along the way, you'll pass the training center for Rochester police and fire units.

The trail ends at a parking area where Route 252A meets Scottsville Road (Route 383). To connect with the next segment of the Genesee Valley Greenway currently requires a 1.7-mile road-walk south on Route 383 then west on Route 252.

Trail Directions
- From the Roundhouse parking area, head north on the paved path toward the Genesee River.
- At the "T," turn left then bear right to head uphill and cross the Waldo J. Nielson Bridge which arches over the Genesee River.
- After the bridge, turn left (NW). (To the right is the Genesee River Trail which is described in *Take Your Bike! Family Rides in the Rochester Area*.)
- At the "T," turn left to head over another bridge. This one spans the Erie Canal. (The former Pennsylvania Railroad bridge is to your right.)
- At 0.3 mile, continue straight (NW) at the next junction. (To the right is the Erie Canalway Trail to Lockport which is also described in *Take Your Bike! Family Rides in the Rochester Area*.)
- Quickly pass another trail to the right. (This is the official Genesee Valley Greenway Trail which was closed when we hiked it but should be open shortly. It merges shortly with the trail you're on.)
- Pass the Police & Fire Academy on your right. The Genesee River is on your left.
- At 1.0 mile, turn right just after the Academy. (Straight ahead dead ends in 0.2 mile.)
- Pass two yellow metal gates.
- At 2.2 miles, reach the Route 383 parking area, next to Gillirmos American Italian Restaurant. Why not stop in for a treat? (To continue south on the Genesee Valley Greenway requires a 1.7 mile road walk. Cross Route 383 and turn left (W) to walk the shoulder. Cross the Conrail railroad tracks. Turn right (W) onto Route 252. The Genesee Valley Greenway crosses Route 252 in 0.5 mile. See the map on page 72.)

Date Hiked: _____

Notes:

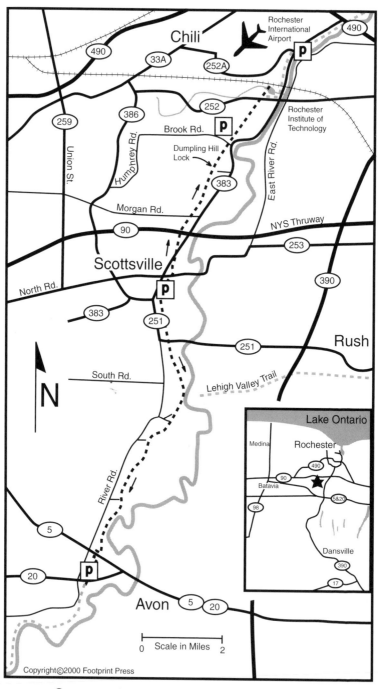

Genesee Valley Greenway - Scottsville

15.
Genesee Valley Greenway
Scottsville

Location: Canawaugus Park, Scottsville

Directions: From the Henrietta exit #44 on the New York State Thruway (Interstate 90), head south on Route 390. At the Route 251 exit, turn right (W) and follow Route 251 to the Canawaugus Park parking lot (on the right just before entering Scottsville).

Alternative Parking: Trail intersection on Brook Road
Trail intersection on Route 20

Hiking Time: 3.5 hours (north)
4.5 hours (south)

Length: 6.6 miles one way (north)
8.4 miles one way (south)

Difficulty: Note: crossing Routes 5 and 383 require short, steep climbs

Surface: Cinder and crushed stone path

Trail Markings: White, metal "Genesee Valley Greenway" signs and yellow metal gates at road crossings

Uses:

Dogs: OK on leash

Admission: Free

Contact: Friends of the Genesee Valley Greenway, Inc.
P.O. Box 42, Mount Morris, NY 14510
(716) 658-2569
http://www.netacc.net/~fogvg

Regional Land Manager
N.Y.S. Department of Environmental Conservation
7291 Coon Road, Bath, NY 14810
(607) 776-2165
http://www.dec.state.ny.us

From Canawaugus Park you can head north for 6.6 miles to the active Conrail tracks north of Route 252. This option takes you past Dumpling Hill Lock #2, one of the best-preserved locks on the Genesee Valley Canal that operated from 1840 to 1878. The canal's original 115 locks were made of either wood, a combination of wood and stone, or all stone. Over

73

Louis D'Amanda sits atop his percheron horse, Matthew. Both enjoy an outing on a multi-use trail.

Percherons are produced by crossing Arabian horses with an old Flemish breed represented now by the Belgian.

the years, the wood rotted and most locks deteriorated or were lost altogether. But this 90-foot-long, 15-foot-wide lock is all stone and well preserved. Each lock had a lock keeper and sometimes a lock house. The Dumpling Hill Lock had a house, which was located west of the canal near Coates Road.

From the north end you can follow Route 252 east, then Route 383 north for 1.7 miles of road-walk then continue on the Genesee Valley Greenway into Genesee Valley Park. This segment is described as Trail #14 on page 70.

You can also head south from Canawaugus Park for 8.4 miles to Route 20. Just before reaching Route 20, it's a steep climb to Route 5 from the trail. Ramps are planned to make the climb easier. This hike is more remote, passing through lush farmlands. See Trail #10 in *Take Your Bike! Family Rides in the Finger Lakes & Genesee Valley Region* for the continuation of Genesee Valley Greenway south of Route 20 for an additional 12.6 miles.

Whichever direction you choose, the trail has an easy-hiking, hard-packed cinder or crushed stone base.

From the parking area at Canawaugus Park, look across to the north side of Oatka Creek to see an old feeder gate for the Genesee Valley Canal. A feeder gate consisted of a lock, dam, and tollhouse.

Trail Directions – North

- Begin by crossing Oatka Creek on the plate girder (former Pennsylvania Railroad) bridge known locally as the "George Bridge." You are heading northeast on the trail.
- Cross Route 253 and pass Rodney Farms, a thoroughbred horse farm, on the right.

- As you approach Route 383, bear right (following the Genesee Valley Greenway sign) and climb a steep hill.
- Climb over the guardrail and cross Route 383 with care, being certain that you can see oncoming traffic far enough ahead for a safe crossing. (A short distance to the left along Route 383 is a small graveyard with the gravestone of Joseph Morgan, a Revolutionary War captain. He is credited with being the first settler in Chili in 1792.)
- Climb over the guardrail on the opposite side of the road and continue downhill to the trail.
- Pass under the New York State Thruway.
- Cross a gravel driveway.
- Cross Morgan Road.
- Pass under two sets of power lines.
- Cross several farm lanes.
- Reach Dumpling Hill Lock.
- Overlook horse farms as you walk high on the rail bed.
- Cross Brook Road at 4.6 miles.
- Pass an underground gas pipeline.
- At 5.6 miles, watch for the "W" carved in a metal post on the right. It signaled the train conductor to blow the whistle as they approached a road crossing.
- Cross Ballantyne Road (Route 252). You are near the airport so don't be startled if a jet rumbles overhead. (To continue on the Genesee Valley Greenway into Genesee Valley Park, turn right and follow Route 252 for 0.5 mile. Then turn left and follow Route 383 north for 1.2 miles. At the intersection with Route 252A, turn right and cross through the parking lot of Gillirmos Restaurant.)
- Pass a wetland on the right.
- You'll see Black Creek on the right as it heads toward the Genesee River. You're actually walking on a culvert where the waters of Black Creek are diverted under what used to be the Genesee Valley Canal.

- The trail ends at 6.6 miles at the active Conrail tracks. (The trail to the right is on private property.) Turn around and retrace your path.

Date Hiked: _____
Notes:

Trail Directions – South

- From the Canawaugus Park parking lot, head southwest, away from "George Bridge."
- Cross several farm field access paths and a private driveway.
- At 1.0 mile, cross Route 251.
- Cross a bridge at 2.1 miles.
- At 2.6 miles, you'll see the old Lehigh Valley Railroad trestle spanning the Genesee River. Someday, this bridge will link the Genesee Valley Greenway to the Lehigh Valley Trail. Also, pass an abandoned gravel pit area on the right (W).
- Cross a farm road.
- Watch carefully to see if you can find the trestle of the abandoned Peanut Branch of the New York Central Railroad. Being a small line earned it the nickname Peanut Branch.
- Pass a beaver pond.
- At 4.2 miles, cross a gated entrance to a farmer's fields labeled with a large "Warning – No Trespassing" sign.
- Cross a buried petroleum pipeline.
- Cross a road that leads to a private farm.
- Cross an underground gas pipeline and several farm lanes.
- At 7.4 miles, pass between the stone trestle of the abandoned Erie Railroad that runs east–west. (There is a path on each side.)
- Reach the steep climb to Route 5 and continue west along the guardrail.
- At the end of the guardrail, cross Route 5 and head east toward a gravel road.
- At the Genesee Valley Greenway sign, head downhill to the trail.
- Pass a quarry on your right and an old segment of the Genesee River to your left. (The Genesee, like most rivers, wanders with time, leaving abandoned channels where an oxbow got cut off from the main channel.)
- Pass through yellow metal gates just before reaching Route 20.

Date Hiked: _____

Notes:

Southeast
Section

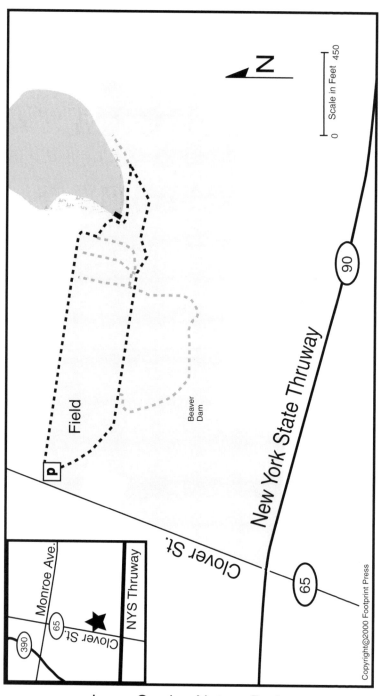

Isaac Gordon Nature Park

16.
Isaac Gordon Nature Park

Location:	Clover Street, Pittsford
Directions:	From Pittsford, head south on Route 65. The Isaac Gordon Nature Park parking area is on the east side of Clover Street (Route 65), just north of the N.Y. State Thruway.

Alternate Parking: None
Hiking Time: 35 minutes
Length: 1.0 mile loop
Difficulty: 👣 👣

Surface: Dirt and mowed-grass paths
Trail Markings: None
Uses:

Dogs: OK on leash
Admission: Free
Contact: Town of Pittsford, Parks and Recreation Department
35 Lincoln Avenue, Pittsford, NY 14534
(716) 381-8420

The Isaac Gordon Foundation and Dr. Jerome Glazer donated the land for this delightful park to the town of Pittsford. The western section is a farm field that the trail circumnavigates. The eastern section is a pond and wetland in a hilly forest. In May the forest floor is dotted with groves of trillium. A raised observation platform affords an unobstructed view of the wetland; great for bird watching. Making a series of loops around the various intersecting paths can extend your enjoyment of this park.

Trail Directions
- From the parking area walk south on the mulched trail. It will take you to a treed tunnel with a canopy of leaves overhead.
- Continue straight, past a trail to the right. (The 0.3-mile path to the right meanders through a mowed field and circles back to meet the treed tunnel. You can extend your hike another 5 minutes by turning right but the field is uneven, difficult to walk, and can be wet.)
- Continue straight through the next intersection.
- Continue straight, past a grassy trail to the left.
- The trail will head uphill and bend left several times, then heads downhill.

- At 0.5 mile, turn left and head downhill. (The path straight ahead dead-ends shortly. It is however, a nice walk through woods on a narrow path along the wetland.)
- Wind through the woods to an observation deck overlooking the wetlands.
- Continue uphill. Turn right (N) when the path comes to a "T."
- Pass two trails off to the left (or loop back to extend your walk) and continue straight to return to the parking area.

Date Hiked: _____

Notes:

Mendon Ponds Park

This is a jewel in the county's park system, filled with lakes, woods, and rolling hills. Mendon Ponds Park is the largest park in Monroe County and was designated a National Natural Landmark because of its unique glacial land forms.

The park's geologic features were formed by the last of four major glaciers that covered the area 12,000 to 14,000 years ago. The glacier reached to the Pennsylvania border and was 5,000 to 10,000 feet thick. As the ice melted, large amounts of sand, rock, and gravel were deposited. Three main geologic features visible in the park today are: kames, eskers, and kettles.

Kames — formed by rivers that flowed on top of the glacier and spilled over the edge depositing soil into huge piles.

KAME

ESKER

Eskers — formed when rivers flowed under the glacier in an ice tunnel. Rocky material accumulated on the tunnel beds, and when the glacier melted, a ridge of rubble remained.

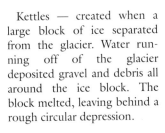

Kettles — created when a large block of ice separated from the glacier. Water running off of the glacier deposited gravel and debris all around the ice block. The block melted, leaving behind a rough circular depression.

KETTLE

People from all over the country come to study "Devil's Bathtub." This kettle is a rare meromictic lake, of which there are only a few in the world. A meromictic lake is a very deep body of water surrounded by high ridges. Because the high ridges prevent the wind from blowing on the water, the lake's water levels never turn over and the motionless surface gives the lake a mirrored effect.

The first inhabitants of this area were the Algonquin, Iroquois, and Seneca Indians who left behind many Indian trails. On July 23, 1687, the Marquis de Denonville's army used the trails to attack the Indians in the region. In his memoirs, Denonville recalls looking down from the top of one of the ridges at "three pretty little lakes." The first reference to Mendon Ponds in our recorded history. The first white settler in the Mendon Ponds area was Joshua Lillie, who is buried on a small plot on Wilmarth Road. The park was dedicated in 1928 and now has 25 to 30 miles of winding trails.

Stop by the nature center for a map on additional trails and information on the glacial geology of the park. The center offers weekly family programs and is open Thursday through Sunday, noon until 4:00 PM, (716) 334-3780.

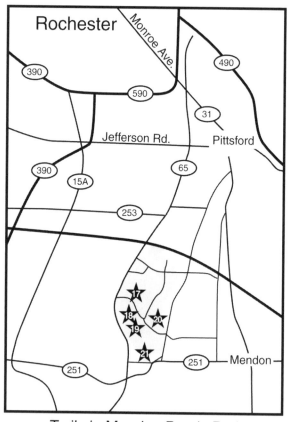

Trails in Mendon Ponds Park

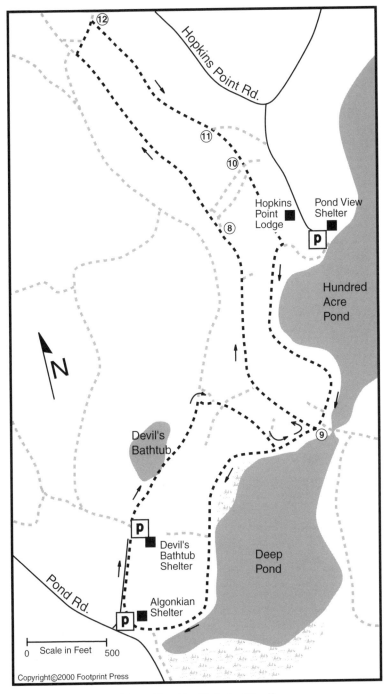

Devil's Bathtub Trail

17.
Devil's Bathtub Trail

Location: Mendon Ponds Park, Mendon
Directions: From Rochester head south on Route 65 (Clover
                   Street). Turn left (E) at the third entrance to Mendon
                   Ponds Park on Pond Road. Turn left just before
                   Algonkian Shelter and park in the Devil's Bathtub
                   Shelter parking area. (When this access road is closed in
                   winter, park at the Algonkian Shelter parking area.)
Alternative Parking: Algonkian Shelter parking area along Pond Road
Hiking Time: 1 hour and 15 minutes
Length: 2.3 mile loop
Difficulty: 👣 👣 👣 👣
                   👣 👣 👣 👣

Surface: Dirt and mulched path
Trail Markings: Some blue numbered signs on posts
Uses:

Dogs: OK on leash
Admission: Free
Contact: Monroe County Parks Department
                   171 Reservoir Avenue
                   Rochester, NY 14620
                   (716) 256-4950

The route described will introduce you to the variety of Mendon Ponds Park. It begins with a descent to Devil's Bathtub kettle pond, nestled in a deep valley. Then you'll climb steeply to the ridge of an esker. Descend off the esker to walk through a wooded forest valley then wander a flat trail along the edge of Hundred Acre Pond and Deep Pond.

Trail Directions
- From the Devil's Bathtub Shelter parking area, walk under the wooden "Mendon NYS-YCC-1989 Devil's Bathtub Trail" sign.
- Descend the wooden stairs and continue straight on the boardwalk with Devil's Bathtub kettle pond to your left.
- Bear right (E) when the trail "Ys" and head uphill.
- Quickly, bear right again and continue uphill.
- Continue straight (SE) through an intersection and head downhill to Deep Pond. (Pass more small trails along the way.)

- At 0.2 mile, reach a "T" and turn left. Deep Pond is now on your right.
- Pass an opening to Deep Pond on the right.
- At the next trail junction, turn left and head uphill. This is a long climb to the ridge of the esker.
- Reach the top of the esker and continue straight on the wide trail.
- Continue straight (N) passing several small trails on both sides.
- At 0.7 mile you'll see junction marker #8 where the trail "Ys." Bear left to continue on the esker ridge.
- Reach a trail intersection at 1.0 mile and turn right (E) to descend off the esker.
- At 1.1 miles, reach junction marker #12 and turn right (SE) to continue downhill.
- Continue straight (S) passing a trail to the left. Junction marker #11 is buried in the bushes at this junction.
- At 1.4 miles continue straight through the intersection marked with junction marker #10 which is also buried in the bushes.
- Quickly pass another trail to the right. Stay on the main trail and head downhill to pond level.
- At the "T," turn right (SW). Hundred Acre Pond is now on your left.
- Pass a small trail to the right.
- At 1.7 miles, continue straight (SW) past a trail to the left that leads between the ponds.
- Pass junction marker #9 and a trail to the right. Continue straight (SW).
- Pass an opening to Deep Pond on the left.
- Pass two trails on the right.
- At 2.1 miles, reach Algonkian Shelter. Turn right and pass the shelter.
- Turn right at the access road, passing a metal yellow gate. Head uphill to the Devil's Bathtub Shelter parking area.

Date Hiked: _____

Notes:

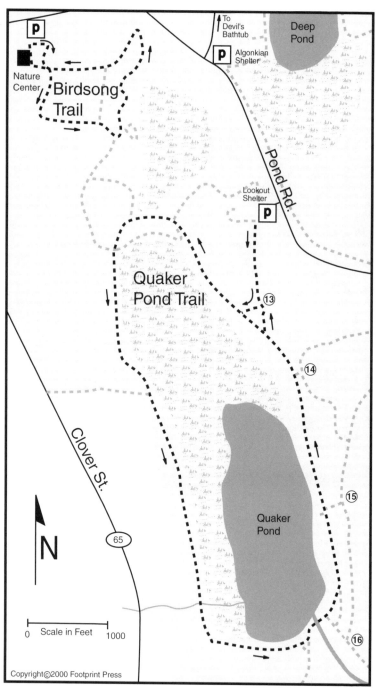

P

To
Devil's
Bathtub

Deep
Pond

P Algonkian
Shelter

Nature
Center

Birdsong
Trail

Pond Rd.

Lookout
Shelter

P

Quaker
Pond Trail

⑬

⑭

Clover St.

N

65

⑮

Quaker
Pond

⑯

0   Scale in Feet   1000

Copyright©2000 Footprint Press

Birdsong Trail & Quaker Pond Trail

18.
Birdsong Trail

Location:	Mendon Ponds Park, Mendon
Directions:	From Rochester, head south on Route 65 (Clover Street). At the third park entrance, turnleft into Mendon Ponds Park on Pond Road. The nature center parking area will be on the right.

Alternative Parking: None
Hiking Time: 35 minutes
Length: 1.1 mile loop
Difficulty: 👣 👣 👣

Surface: Dirt path
Trail Markings: Signs at intersections
Uses: 🚶

Dogs: Pets are NOT allowed
Admission: Free
Contact: Monroe County Parks Department
171 Reservoir Avenue
Rochester, NY 14620
(716) 256-4950

As the name indicates, many birds populate this area especially black-capped chickadees. These friendly, curious creatures will fly right up to you, and if you have sunflower seeds, they will eat out of your hand. For part of the journey, you'll walk an old farm lane as evidenced by the large trees that line the trail. Some of them are labeled, making this walk an arbor study.

Black-capped chickadees eat from your hand.

Trail Directions
- From the trellis walkway, turn left on Old Orchard Trail.
- The trail will bend right.
- At the "T," turn left onto an old farm lane.

- Quickly turn right onto Birdsong Trail. (Notice the stone walls that line both sides of the trail. Imagine the farmer who had to clear these from his fields.)
- At 0.2 mile the trail bends left at a sign about animal tracks.
- Turn right at the "T."
- Reach a "Y" at 0.4 mile and bear left on Birdsong Trail.
- Pass two small trails to the right. (They lead to a small swamp with an observation deck and benches.)
- Pass an observation deck at 0.5 mile.
- Pass a bench and head downhill beside a wooden railing. There's a second bench at the bottom of the hill.
- Reach a "T" at 0.9 mile and turn right (NW).

Dorothy Murphy and Joyce Connor stroll along Birdsong Trail.

- Continue straight, passing a trail to the left then another to the right.
- Pass an observation platform on the left and bear right on a paved path toward the nature center building.
- Pass a hummingbird garden, a butterfly garden, and an herb garden.
- Turn right to head under the trellis and return to the parking area.

Date Hiked: _____

Notes:

19.
Quaker Pond Trail

Location:	Mendon Ponds Park, Mendon
Directions:	Take Clover Street (Route 65) south to Mendon Ponds Park. Turn left (E) at the third entrance to the park on Pond Road. Pass the nature center and Algonkian Shelter. Park at the Lookout Shelter parking area.

Alternative Parking: The nature center parking area

Hiking Time:	1.3 hours
Length:	2.5 mile loop
Difficulty:	👞 👞 👞 👞
Surface:	Mowed-grass and dirt path
Trail Markings:	Some signs and numbered posts at intersections
Uses:	
Dogs:	Pets are NOT allowed
Admission:	Free
Contact:	Monroe County Parks Department 171 Reservoir Avenue Rochester, NY 14620 (716) 256-4950

This trail offers an easy stroll on a wide path. Cattails and bushes are encroaching on the pond, but water is still visible at the southern end. Waterfowl and lily pads are plentiful in the remaining pond. In spring and winter it's a fun place to identify animal tracks (deer, raccoon, beaver, etc.) in the mud. On a winter walk we watched a mink scurry across the ice. In July we've enjoyed grazing on the raspberries and blackberries that line the trail.

You can make the hike longer by combining this walk with Birdsong Trail (#18) or Mendon Grasslands Trail (#21).

Trail Directions
- From Lookout Shelter parking area, head west on the gravel trail. Immediately turn left (S).
- At the "Y," (junction marker #13) bear right (W).
- At 0.2 mile, reach a "T." Turn right (W).
- At 0.4 mile, pass a trail to the left. (It's a boardwalk through the swamp and can be taken as a shortcut.)

- Bear left as you pass a trail to the right.
- Pass a bench and cross a small wooden bridge over the swamp outlet.
- At 0.5 mile, a trail to the right leads to the nature center. Continue straight (W).
- Continue straight through a trail intersection.
- At 0.8 mile, pass a trail to the right. (It leads to Clover Street.)

Sunset over Quaker Pond.

- Cross a culvert at 1.4 miles.
- At 1.5 miles the trail bends left (SE).
- Pass a trail to the right.
- At the "T," turn left (E). Finally you'll see water.
- Cross a wooden bridge over the pond outlet at 1.7 miles. (Notice that beavers had once dammed this waterway.)
- At the "Y," bear left (NE).
- Pass a trail to the right at 1.8 miles.
- At 2.0 miles pass a trail to the left then quickly pass a trail to the right.
- At 2.3 miles reach trail junction #14. Continue straight.
- Cross a small wooden bridge.
- At 2.3 miles, bear right (N) at the "Y" to head back to Lookout Hill and Pond Road.
- Reach a "T" at junction marker #13 at 2.4 miles and turn right (NE).
- At the last "T" turn right to return to the parking area.

Date Hiked: _____

Notes:

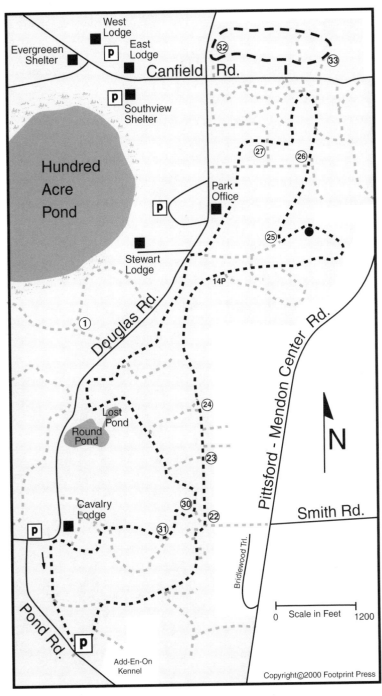

Eastern Ski Trail & Pine Forest Loop

20.
Eastern Ski Trail

Location: Mendon Ponds Park, Mendon
Directions: From Route 65, turn east into Mendon Ponds Park on Pond Road. Pass Douglas Road and park in the "Horse Trailer Parking" area on the north side of Pond Road, just before Add-En-On Kennel.
Alternative Parking: The parking area at the corner of Pond Road and Douglas Road
Along Canfield Road, east of Douglas Road
Hiking Time: 3 hours
Length: 5.7 mile loop
Difficulty:
Surface: Dirt and mulched path
Trail Markings: Not well marked, some blue and white metal signs on wooden posts at trail junctions
Uses:
Dogs: OK on leash
Admission: Free
Contact: Monroe County Parks Department
171 Reservoir Avenue, Rochester, NY 14620
(716) 256-4950

This wide, distinctively hilly path is used for cross-country skiing in the winter and hiking and horseback riding the rest of the year. The trail is well maintained with mulch in heavy wear areas making it an easy-to-hike horse trail. You're likely to encounter horses on a nice weekend day and need to be alert for fresh horse droppings year-round.

There are many opportunities to shorten the loop hike, if you wish. Simply refer to the map.

The trail described follows a portion of the Mendon Ponds Tree Walk which was established by Erik Rexo, the staff of Mendon Ponds Park, and Boy Scout Troop 167 of Pittsford. Numbers on posts refer to the following trees:

24. Common Catalpa: This easily identifiable tree has long twisting limbs with large heart-shaped leaves 6 to 13 inches in size. The leaves emit a foul odor when crushed. Beautiful, fragrant clustered flowers appear in May-July. Interesting "string-bean" fruits 18 to 20 inches long decorate the tree in fall. It grows rapidly, showing tolerance to many soil conditions, temperature, and moisture ranges.

23. Red Maple: A true fall dazzler that adds those deep reds and yellows to the fall foliage. These trees survive in many varied areas of the park, from esker top to swamp bottom and everything in between.

22. Red Oak: A majority of the hardwoods in the park are mature red oak stands. A relatively fast growing tree able to reach towering heights of over 100 feet. The majority of oak woods in the park are well over 100 years old. It's called red oak because in the spring the newly unfolding leaves are red in color.

21. Black Locust: This fast-growing, thorny tree has adapted to many areas in the park. These trees become ragged and scraggly with age. The flowers are extremely fragrant and flow on 4 to 8 inch long racemes. The wood is rot resistant and is used for posts.

20. Honey Suckle: There are over 80 species of honey suckle. They are a tough invasive pioneer plant that seeds readily. They grow in many shapes and sizes. Some are extremely fragrant. They grow rampant throughout Mendon Ponds.

19. Staghorn Sumac: Large pinnately compound leaves with 13 to 27 leaflets combined with a large red seed head and furry looking bark make this an easy tree to identify. The scraggly looking tree has picturesque branches that resemble the horns of a deer.

18. White Ash: This is a brilliant fall color tree not as large as some, but has the potential to reach 100 feet in optimum conditions. Unfortunately, this species is threatened by a significant list of health problems; their numbers continue to decline.

17. Black Walnut: This particular tree can get quite large — up to 125 feet high. The wood is extremely valuable and is used in the finest furniture. Walnuts are allelopathic, their dropped fruit makes the area under the tree uninhabitable for most plants due to growth inhibitors in the fruit.

6. Pignut Hickory: This large tree can reach 80+ feet in height. The nuts are an available food source for wildlife. The wood is used for smoking meats and making tool handles. A very valuable tree that helps balance our native woodlands. Identifiable by its pinnately compounded five leaflet leaves.

5. Douglas Fir: A confusing tree for some arborists because there are two main varieties. The first being the coastal Douglas fir which can attain heights of 300 feet; a huge resource for commercial timber. The second being the Rocky Mountain Douglas fir which grows to 130 feet tall. It's the ornamental variety and the variety that we have in the park. A favorite Christmas tree due to its camphor smell and needles that don't readily fall off.

Mendon Pond Park's Eastern Ski Trail.

Trail Directions

- From the parking area with the brown "Horse Trailer Parking" sign, head north on a farm lane, passing a single wooden rail fence on your right. (A trail to the right along the fence line goes to Add-En-On Kennel.)
- Continue uphill on the main path avoiding the cut-off on the left.
- Go up and over the crest of the hill and cross through a valley.
- At the "Y" junction, bear left and go up the hill, staying on the wide, mulched trail.
- At the top of the hill is a tiny loop with a view and picnic table. Continue north along the top of an esker.
- Continue straight (N) past a trail to the left. (It's a small loop trail.)
- At 0.8 mile, reach a "T" and turn right. Notice the sign "Duck Hill" on the tree to your right. (Left is the return of the small loop trail.)
- At junction marker #22, continue straight, following the wide trail. (Note: A horse trail parallels and crosses the hiking trail a few times.)
- At the top of the next hill at junction marker #23, continue straight, up and down several hills to junction marker #24. (You'll pass several small trails to the right on your way to marker #24.)
- Bear right and ascend and then descend an esker.
- Continue straight, downhill at the junction marked with a 14P orienteering stake.
- Pass the snow groomer turn around.
- Continue straight (SE) through a small trail intersection.
- Stay on the wide path as it climbs a steep hill and leads to the water tower at 2.2 miles. (Several small trails lead from the main trail along the way.)
- The path continues on the opposite side of the tower using a gravel road for a short distance.

- At junction marker #25 turn right (N) down a wood chip path. (Begin watching for trees labeled by numbered signs.)
- At 2.6 miles, reach junction marker #26 and bear right.
- Pass a small trail on the right.
- At the top of the hill continue straight past a trail to the right.
- For the next several unmarked junctions, always bear left.
- As you begin to walk west, notice trees that were planted in rows.
- At 3.1 miles, reach junction marker #27 and continue straight (W).
- Continue straight through an unmarked junction. (Look for tree markers #5 and #6 near this junction.)
- Cross the lawn behind the park office building and reenter woods.
- Bear right at the "Y," and turn right on the gravel road (which leads left to the cement water tower). Turn left at the gated fence.
- After several hills enter a grass area following the line of the woods and reenter the woods to the left after 1,000 feet.
- Cross another grass area.
- At the "Y" bear right heading toward Douglas Road.
- Merge with a trail from the left.
- Follow trail as it bears left, then up a hill to a sharp right.
- Trail bends left as you approach Douglas Road.
- At the picnic area, bear left around Lost Pond, returning into the woods.
- At 4.6 miles, reach junction marker #30 and continue straight. (The path is leaf covered and the terrain is gentle through this area.)
- Pass a small trail intersection.
- At junction marker #31 turn right (W), uphill. (The terrain gets hilly again.)
- At the next junction, bear right to follow the widest trail.
- A small trail will come in from the left then reach a "Y." Bear left on the dirt trail.
- Pass a small trail on the right.
- At 5.3 miles, the trail bears left near Douglas Road and heads uphill.
- Continue straight past a trail to the left to return to the parking area.

Date Hiked: _____
Notes:

Bonus: Pine Forest Loop Trail

This is a delightful 30 minutes (1.2 miles) through a mature pine forest using a wide country lane. The trail makes a big rectangle with a shortcut trail through the center.

Trail Directions

- Park on the north side of Canfield Road between Douglas Road and Mendon Center Road. A yellow pipe gate set back near the woods is the entrance.
- Walk to the opening in the woods on the north side of the road.
- Since this is a loop, you can take the trail in either direction.

Date Hiked: _____
Notes:

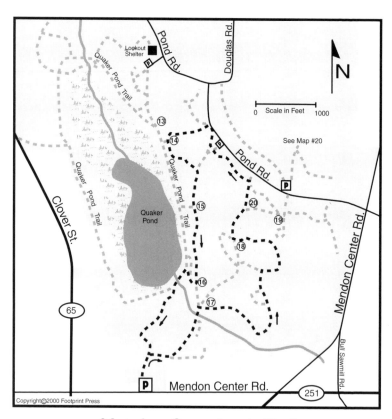

Mendon Grasslands Trail

21.
Mendon Grasslands Trail

Location: Mendon Ponds Park, Mendon
Directions: From Route 65 turn east onto Mendon Center Road. The parking area is 0.3 mile from the corner. Look for a small brown and white horse sign.
Alternative Parking: Along Pond Road
Hiking Time: 1.25 hours
Length: 3.4 mile loop
Difficulty:

Surface: mowed-grass and dirt trails
Trail Markings: Some numbered sign posts
Uses:

Dogs: Pets are NOT allowed
Admission: Free
Contact: Monroe County Parks Department
171 Reservoir Avenue, Rochester, NY 14620
(716) 256-4950

Enter Mendon Ponds Park through its back door into a secluded area of rolling hills, young forests, scrub brush, and large grass fields. Horses are allowed on most of this route but the trails are in good shape for hiking and are wide enough to avoid the horse trough where it does exist.

You'll walk through fields of tall grasses and along Quaker Pond to the serenade of Canada geese, and evidence of beaver activity. We walked this trail in early spring when ice still covered portions of the pond and were treated to mink playing on the ice and a blue heron patiently waiting to catch his dinner. Be sure to bring some sunflower seeds. The Chickadees lay in wait along this trail, expecting a hand-out. They're bold enough to land on your hand to get the seeds.

Trail Directions
- From the parking area on Mendon Center Road, head north on an eight-foot-wide mowed path.
- Enter the woods and bear right at the "Y" on the horse trail.
- Leave the woods and bear left, passing a trail to the right. Stay on the wide trail.
- Pass another small trail to the right.
- At 0.4 mile, cross Quaker Pond outlet.

- At junction marker #17 take a sharp right, heading east.
- At 0.7 mile, pass the entrance to a small, high-water loop trail on the left. (If the trail has been muddy, take this high-water route to the left.)
- Pass the return of the high-water loop.
- At 1.0 mile reach a "T" and turn right (E).
- Turn right (N) at junction marker #18.
- Continue straight (N) through junction marker #20.
- At the next intersection (shortly before the road), turn left (NW) and head uphill. Notice the remains of an old brick outhouse at the top of the hill in a grove of trees.
- Pass a trail to a parking area on the right then quickly bear right past two trails to the left. You're now heading north.
- Walk along the edge of Pond Road for about 50 feet then turn left (SW) into a gully.
- Pass a small pond on the right.
- Take the first left (SE) before the "No Horses" sign on junction marker #14 and head uphill. This is a good place to stop and feed Chickadees from your hand.
- At 2.3 miles, reach a "T" and turn right (SW).
- At the next junction, bear left and pass junction marker #15 hidden in brush to the left.
- At the next junction, turn right (W). (If you go to far you'll reach junction marker #16. Just turn right & backtrack.)
- Quickly pass through an intersection and continue straight (W) toward Quaker Pond.
- At the "T," turn left (W) along the edge of Quaker Pond. Notice all the trees cut by beavers as you approach the outlet bridge.
- Cross the wooden outlet bridge. You've come 2.8 miles.
- Continue straight (S), past a trail to the right.
- Pass a barricade and continue straight to return to the parking area.

Date Hiked: _____

Notes:

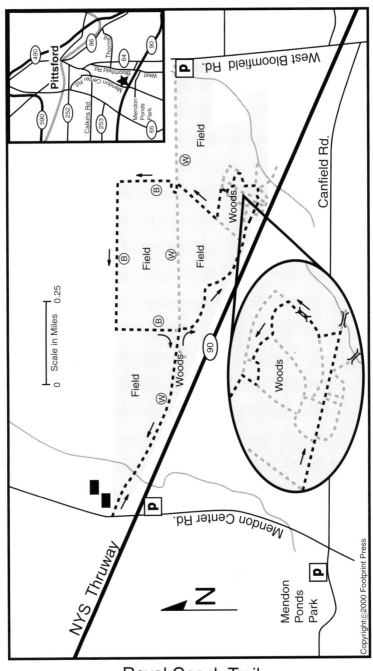

Royal Coach Trail

22.
Royal Coach Trail

Location: Mendon Center Road, Pittsford

Directions: From Pittsford, head south on Route 64. Bear right onto Mendon Center Road. Parking is not allowed at the trailhead. Park along Mendon Center Road just south of the NYS Thruway overpass.

Alternative Parking: Along Canfield Road in Mendon Ponds Park
    A gravel pull-off area along West Bloomfield Road

Hiking Time: 75 minutes

Length: 2.2 mile loop

Difficulty: 👣 👣 👣

Surface: Mowed-grass and dirt trails

Trail Markings: White and blue blazes

Uses:

Dogs: OK on leash

Admission: Free

Contact: Pittsford Parks & Recreation
    35 Lincoln Avenue, Pittsford, NY 14534
    (716) 248-6280

Royal Coach gets its name from Walnut Hill Farms which abuts the property on the eastern edge. Each August, Walnut Hill is the meeting place for elaborate horse drawn coaches and carts. They host a competition of driving skill and give awards for costuming and restoration of the old carriages. Watching the competition is a fun way to spend a summer weekend day. The horses and carts use the trails through the woods at the eastern end of this property for their time trials.

On a fall day, while walking on Royal Coach Trail, we were treated to a rare sight. A young gray fox pranced in front of us and pounced several times as he hunted for mice in the fields. We were down wind so it was only when we crept forward to get a better look that he took note of us and bounded away.

The trail begins with a climb past farm fields. Once at the top of the hill you enter a maze of trails in a deep woods. This is where the driving competition takes place. Recently a sculptor has been busy in the area. On our last hike, the woods had sprouted a fox and a pine tree carved into the trunks of downed trees. The return winds downhill around fields.

The drone of Thruway noise is never out of earshot but the splendor of hilltop vistas makes it bearable. In fall, the reds, bronzes, yellows, and greens of the trees contrast sharply with the beige carpet of dying corn-stalks. This is indeed a pretty place to go for a stroll.

Trail Directions
- Follow Mendon Center Road north, passing under the NYS Thruway bridge.
- Less than 0.1 mile from the Thruway bridge, turn right (E) at the green "Town of Pittsford Parkland Restrictions" sign.

Boulder leads Dave Wright, Dave Coleman, and Rich Freeman on a fall hike on Royal Coach Trail.

- Walk east on a farm lane. It parallels the Thruway and heads uphill.
- Pass another green sign at 0.3 mile as a woods begins to your right.
- A small path to the right leads into woods. Continue straight until a gap in the woods on your right. (A wooden sign shows that the white trail continues straight and the blue trail turns left.)
- Turn right and follow the mowed-grass trail around the edge of a field toward the Thruway. (You're on an unmarked trail.)
- Parallel the thruway then proceed straight (E).
- Pass a grassy trail to the left and continue straight (E) entering the woods at 0.7 mile. (The woods are full of many intersecting trails.)
- Continue straight on the wide path. (You'll pass a trail to the left, then a trail to the right marked with a "Camper's Path" sign.)
- Keep going straight. (You'll pass a trail on the left then 3 trails to the right. The third right leads over a small bridge.)
- At 0.8 mile turn left (N) and head uphill toward a wooden cut-out of a leaning man. (If you miss this turn you'll cross a bridge over a small creek. This is private property so turn around.)
- Reach a "T" and turn right (NE).
- Cross a wooden bridge then bear left to stay in the woods. (Straight leads to a field.)
- At 0.9 mile, reach a "Y." Bear right (N) and pass the carved fox.
- Reach a "T." Turn left and follow the trail as it winds through the woods. (Right leads to a field.)
- Reach another "T." This time turn right (N) to leave the woods. (Left passes the pine tree carving.)

101

- At the field, turn left and follow the edge of the field (NW).
- At 1.1 miles, reach a wide "T" and turn right (NE) on a wide grass strip between fields.
- Reach a "T" and gas line post #85. Turn left (NW). (Right leads to West Bloomfield Road.)
- Quickly turn right (N) on the blue-blazed trail. (The trail winds through wooded hedge rows.)
- Bear left twice, following the blue blazes, then head downhill.
- At 1.6 miles, bear left again then head uphill.
- Reach a wide mowed "T" at 1.7 miles and turn right (NW) between the woods and a field.
- Follow the farm road back down to Mendon Center Road.
- Turn left to return to your car.

Date Hiked: _____

Notes:

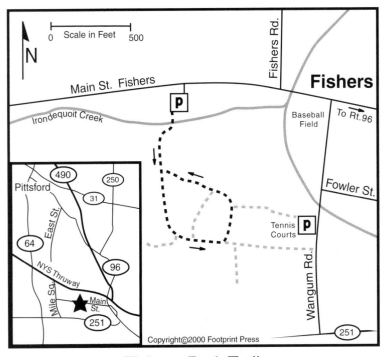

Fishers Park Trail

23.
Fishers Park Trail

Location:	Fishers Park, Main Street Fishers
Directions:	From Route 96, head west on Main Street Fishers, just south of the Thruway. The Fishers Park parking area will be on the left, past Wangum Road.

Alternate Parking: At the tennis courts on Wangum Road
Hiking Time: 45 minutes
Length: 0.7 mile loop
Difficulty: 👣 👣 👣

Surface: Dirt path
Trail Markings: None
Uses: 🚶

Dogs: OK
Admission: Free
Contact: Town of Victor
85 East Main Street, Victor, NY 14564
(716) 924-7141

Fishers Park was part of the original Fisher homestead. Long ago, white-washed stones spelling out "Fishers" were placed on the hill to help early airplane pilots find their way to Rochester. Some white stones can still be found on the hill above the present day tennis courts.

This small, quiet park offers picnic tables and charcoal grills at the Main Street entrance, a baseball field at the corner, and tennis courts off Wangum Road. Fisherman frequent the banks of Irondequoit Creek.

The trail described will take you across the Irondequoit Creek valley and up the facing hillside, deep within a peaceful woods. Side trails lead to private lands. While it may be tempting to venture beyond the park, please respect the landowners rights and stay within the 37.5-acre park.

Trail Directions
• From the Fishers Park parking area, head southwest and cross the large bridge over Irondequoit Creek.
• Cross two smaller bridges.
• At 0.2 mile, pass a small trail to the left. (It will be part of your return loop.)
• The trail gradually climbs out of the valley.

Historical photo of painted stones helping early pilots find their way to Rochester. (Photo courtesy of Larry Fisher.)

- Pass a trail on the right. It may be difficult to see.
- Pass a trail on the left at 0.3 mile.
- Turn left at the next junction.
- At 0.4 mile, pass a trail on the right. (It leads to the tennis courts.)
- Soon you'll reach another junction and bear right to head downhill, back into the valley.
- At 0.5 mile, reach a "T." Turn right (N) and continue downhill to the parking area.

Date Hiked: _____

Notes:

Ganondagan State Historic Site

Once a major seventeenth-century Seneca town and its palisaded granary, Ganondagan is the only historic site, under the auspices of New York State Office of Parks, Recreation and Historic Preservation, that is dedicated to Native Americans. The town and its associated burial grounds on Boughton Hill were designated a National Historic Landmark in 1964. Fort Hill, the site of the town's granary, was placed on the National Register of Historic Places in 1966 because it was part of the French campaign of destruction in 1687. The Marquis de Denonville, Governor General of New France, led an army of 3,000 men from Canada against the Seneca in July, 1687 in an effort to annihilate the Seneca and eliminate them as competitors in the international fur trade.

The Seneca recall a much earlier time period, when a man referred to as the Peacemaker journeyed to their territory and met a woman known as Mother of Nations or Peace Mother. The Seneca know Ganondagan as the "Town of Peace," and revere and protect the burial site of the Mother of Nations near here.

Interpretive signs on the three main trails within Ganondagan teach the significance of plant life for the Seneca, Seneca customs and beliefs, features of the 30 acre granary at Fort Hill, and the events that took place at the granary. On July 14, 1987, Ganondagan was dedicated — 300 years to the day after Denonville destroyed life at Ganondagan.

In 1997 and 1998 a full-scale bark longhouse was constructed at Ganondagan based on extensive research of oral, archaeological, and historical records. The 65-foot long, 20-foot wide structure is stocked with

The Seneca Indian longhouse at Ganondagan.

106

artifacts and displays, showing not only how the Seneca lived, but their governmental and spiritual philosophies as well. When the peaceful Seneca inhabited Ganondagan, up to 20 families could have lived in each longhouse. Ganondagan was the largest Seneca town known to have existed. In the 17th century it had over 150 longhouses and approximately 4,500 residents. Hours that the longhouse is open for viewing vary throughout the year. Call (716) 924-5848 for the current schedule.

The visitor center at Ganondagan features an exhibit describing the Seneca clan system, a display of works by Seneca artists, and a twenty-seven minute video about the history of Ganondagan. The visitor center and gift shop are open May 15 through October 31, Wednesday through Sunday, 9 AM to 5 PM.

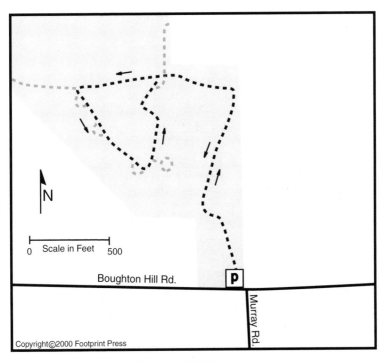

Fort Hill Trail

24.
Fort Hill Trail

Location: Boughton Hill Road (County Road 41), Victor

Directions: From Rochester, head south on Route 64, through
                       Mendon. Turn east on Boughton Hill Road. The grass
                       parking area for Fort Hill will be on the left (north)
                       side of Boughton Hill Road near the corner of Murray
                       Road.

Alternative Parking: None

Hiking Time: 30 minutes to hike (1 hour to hike & read the signs)

Length: 1.0 mile loop

Difficulty: 🥾 🥾 🥾

Surface: Dirt and mowed-grass paths

Trail Markings: Some wooden "trail" signs

Uses: 🚶

Dogs: OK on leash

Admission: Free

Contact: Ganondagan State Historic Site
                       P.O. Box 239, 1488 Victor-Holcomb Road
                       Victor, NY 14564-0239
                       (716) 924-5848

The Fort Hill Trail takes you to the top of a plateau with sweeping views of valleys and hillsides across Victor. This was once the site of the picketed granary for Ganondagan where the winter supply of corn was stored. Forty interpretive signs give first-hand accounts of the mass destruction of the granary by the French campaign of 1687.

Trail Directions
- From the parking area head uphill (N) on the mowed path.
- Turn right and enter the woods through wooden fence posts.
- At 0.2 mile, cross a boardwalk. (To your left note the marsh area, once a spring used by the Seneca.)
- Continue up a steep hill on a dirt path.
- At 0.3 mile, emerge to a mowed field at the top of the hill. (A small trail to the right leads to private property.)

Looking south from atop Fort Hill.

- Head straight into the field, passing two mowed paths to the left. (The mowed path will make a loop around the top of the plateau. Follow signs to stay on the main trail.)
- Reach the edge of the plateau facing west at 0.4 mile. The trail bends left (S). (In addition to reading the interpretive signs along the way, sit and enjoy the views of farmland in the valley below.)
- At 0.6 mile, enter woods then emerge back to the field's edge.
- At the end of the loop, turn right at the "T" and retrace your steps down the same trail to the parking area.

Date Hiked: _____
Notes:

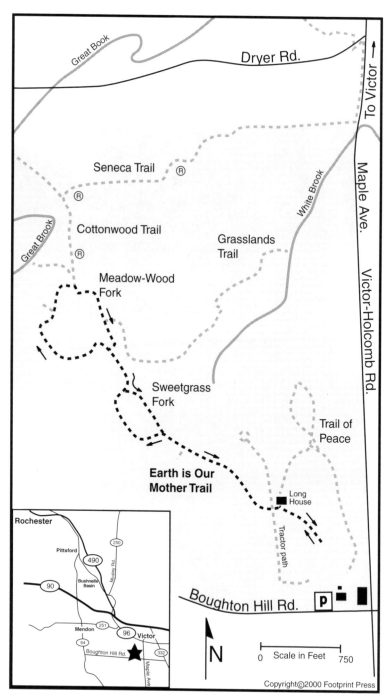

Earth is Our Mother Trail

25.
Earth Is Our Mother Trail

Location:	Ganondagan State Historic Site, Boughton Hill Road, Victor
Directions:	From Route 96 in Victor, turn south on Maple Avenue then west on Boughton Hill Road. Ganondagan parking lot is on Boughton Hill Road near the corner of Victor-Holcomb Road

Alternative Parking: None
Hiking Time: 1.0 hour
Length: 1.9 mile loop
Difficulty: 👣 👣 👣

Surface: Dirt path with boardwalks
Trail Markings: Some wooden trail signs
Uses:

Dogs:	OK on leash
Admission:	Free
Contact:	Ganondagan State Historic Site
	P.O. Box 239, 1488 Victor-Holcomb Road
	Victor, NY 14564-0239
	(716) 924-5848

From the parking area of Ganondagan State Historic Site you have two choices for hikes. Stay on top of the hill and walk the mowed-grass paths of the Trail of Peace through open field for an easy 0.4-mile loop or head into the woods for the more challenging Earth is Our Mother Trail. Or, combine the two. The Earth is Our Mother Trail is described below.

Trail Directions
- From the parking area head north across a mowed-grass area toward an interpretive sign.
- Turn left down the 6-foot mowed path following the Trail of Peace signs.
- At 0.2 mile, pass between a flower garden and the longhouse.
- Continue straight heading into a high brush woods. An interpretive sign will identify this as the "Ethnobotanical Trail."
- The trail descends two flights of steps.
- Cross a boardwalk (wet area in spring).

- Continue straight, past a trail to the left which leads to an interpretive sign.
- At 0.5 mile, cross another boardwalk.
- At the intersection turn left (NW). (Straight is part of the return leg of the hike.)
- At the next junction, turn left (N) again.
- Cross three boardwalks
- At the junction continue straight (W).
- At 0.8 mile, cross a boardwalk.
- Pass a trail to the left which leads to an interpretive sign.
- At the junction turn right (SE). (Note: If you wish to extend your hike, turn left. A trail to the left in 50 feet leads to Great Brook, a beautiful cascading stream. Or, straight at this junction takes you via the Cottonwood Trail to Victor Hiking Trail's 5.8-mile long Seneca Trail. See page 113.)
- Exit the woods to a mowed-grass path through scrub bushes.
- At 1.2 miles, continue straight where a trail enters from the left. (This is the Grassland Trail which is a 1-mile linear trail.)
- Trail reenters woods.
- At the junction, turn left (SE) and cross three boardwalks.
- At the "T" turn left (E) uphill.
- At 1.4 miles, reach an intersection and continue straight ahead (S).
- Cross a boardwalk.
- Emerge to a scrub brush field.
- Pass a trail to the right which leads to an interpretive sign.
- Cross a boardwalk.
- At 1.6 miles, climb two flights of stairs.
- Emerge onto the mowed-grass trail. Pass the longhouse. Continue straight then bear right to return to the parking area.

Date Hiked: _____
Notes:

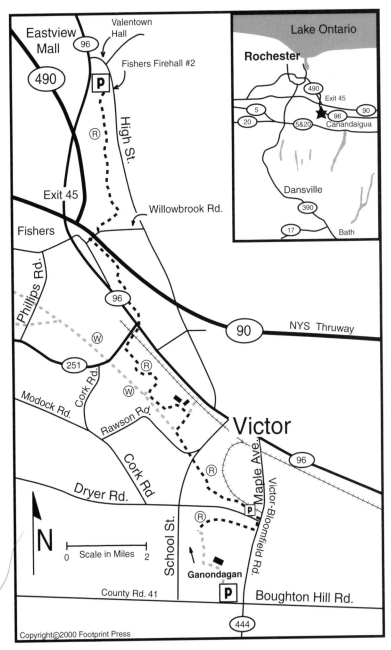

Seneca Trail

26.
Seneca Trail

Location:	Victor, Ontario County
Directions:	Head south on Route 96. In Victor, turn south on Maple Avenue (also called Victor-Bloomfield Road and State Route 444). Turn right (W) on Boughton Hill Road (County Road 41). The parking area for Ganondagan State Historic Site is on Boughton Hill Road, near the corner of Victor-Bloomfield Road.

Alternative Parking: Fishers Firehall on the south side of High Street, Victor (0.25 mile south of Valentown Museum) RG&E Substation on Dryer Road

Hiking Time:	3 hours
Length:	5.8 miles one way
Difficulty:	👣 👣 👣
Surface:	Mowed-grass and dirt trails
Trail Markings:	Red blazes and diamond-shaped, red metal markers
Uses:	🚶
Dogs:	OK
Admission:	Free
Contact:	Victor Hiking Trails
	85 East Main Street, Victor, NY 14564-1397
	(716) 234-8226
	http://www.ggw.org/freenet/v/vht/

This trail is steeped in history and is a wonder of diverse terrain. The journey begins at Ganondagan State Historic Site, once the home of a thriving seventeenth-century Seneca Indian village. See page 106 for additional information on Ganondagan State Historic Site.

From Ganondagan, this trail winds through Victor, passing through Ambush Valley. In 1687 when the Marquis de Denonville and his soldiers came to Ganondagan, most of the Seneca warriors were in Illinois fighting the French. The few who remained attempted to ambush Denonville's army in this narrow valley, but they were significantly outnumbered.

Seneca Trail traverses wooded hills, crosses shrub fields, passes through wetlands, and follows two abandoned rail lines for part of its path. One was the Rochester and Auburn Railroad. The other was an electric trolley line which connected Rochester and Canandaigua before the advent of our interstate highway system. Much of Route 490 utilizes the old trolley bed. At one point along Seneca Trail, the hiker is treated to a view of the Rochester skyline in the distance.

Seneca Trail was built and is maintained by the volunteer organization Victor Hiking Trails. They offer guided hikes on a variety of area trails on the 2nd Saturday of each month. The guided hikes are free and open to the public. Call the VHT hotline (716-234-8226) for the current hike schedule.

Trail Directions
- From the Ganondagan parking area, head northwest across the grass toward the longhouse.
- Pass a brown and yellow "Trail of Peace" sign.
- Pass a perennial garden and the longhouse. The trail continues behind the silver and black "Ethnobotanical Trail" sign, west of the longhouse.
- Head downhill on steps.
- Cross a boardwalk.
- Pass a trail to the left. It's a short side trail to an interpretive sign.
- Cross another boardwalk.
- At an intersection, walk straight (N) where the orange trail signpost is pointing.
- Bear right (N) at a "Y."
- Cross a boardwalk.
- At a trail junction, turn right (N) following the orange trail signpost, heading uphill.
- Emerge from the woods onto a mowed-grass trail. Continue straight past a trail to the right.
- Pass a sign for "Meadow – Wood Fork."
- Re-enter the woods.
- At a "T," turn right (N).
- Pass a trail to the left, staying straight past a "Cottonwood Trail" sign.
- Climb a hill. Eventually a creek will be far below on your left.
- Watch for a trail junction and turn right onto the red-marked Seneca Trail. (The trail straight ahead dead-ends on a high point.)
- The terrain continues to be hilly.
- Exit the woods and walk through a shrub field, following red blazes.
- At Maple Ave. (Victor-Bloomfield Road) turn left (N) and follow the road to Dryer Road.
- Turn left (W) onto Dryer Road.
- Shortly, turn right into the gravel parking area of the RG&E Substation.
- Continue to the northwest corner of the parking area, cross grass, and reenter woods following the red blazed trail.
- Cross a bridge over Great Brook then climb a steep hill.

- Descend the hill. When the trail nears Great Brook, turn right to continue following the red blazed trail.
- The vegetation becomes shrub field.
- At a swale cut in the hill,watch carefully for the trail to head left into the woods. Turn left and head to the top of the hill.
- Emerge into a shrub field and head downhill.
- At the base of the hill, turn left onto the abandoned Auburn Railroad bed.
- Cross School Street.
- Cross Rawson Road.
- At the next junction, turn right (E) on a mowed-grass trail. (White-blazed Auburn Trail continues straight.)
- Enter the woods.
- Pass the historic village artifacts (also known as a dump) to your right.

A group on a guided hike sponsored by Victor Hiking Trails.

- Watch for a trail to the left. Turn left (W). (Straight leads to Route 96 near BitsQuick Café. Not long ago this section of trail was under water, compliments of some industrious beavers. The beavers have moved on and the water level is once again low, allowing clear passage on the trail.)
- Pass abandoned metal and brick buildings on your right.
- Cross several bridges and boardwalks while passing through a wetland area.
- As you exit the woods, notice the horsetail on both sides of the trail. You're now walking on a raised strip which is the abandoned trolley bed. (If leaves are off the trees, you can see the Auburn Trail running parallel to the left.)
- Cross logs over a stream.
- Reach a "T." Turn right and cross a wooden bridge. (Left connects to the Auburn Trail.)
- Cross a boardwalk and corduroy trail.
- Cross three wooden bridges. Watch for golf balls from Auburn Creek Golf Range between bridges 2 and 3.
- Emerge from the woods and cross a small wooden bridge.
- Turn left onto the driveway of Auburn Creek Golf Range.
- At Route 251, turn right.

- Cross Route 96, looking for the red marker on a post. You've come 3.7 miles.
- Follow the washed-out old dirt road uphill.
- Part way up the hill, turn left (NW) off the road. Cross a small stream.
- Pass conglomerate rocks, cross a farm road, and continue straight through a field.
- Pass a small trail to the right.
- Enter Ambush Valley. Watch for poison ivy. Head uphill at the end of the valley.
- Cross a gravel road (may be recently paved) and enter woods. Turn left (N) parallel to the Thruway.
- At Willowbrook Road, turn right (E) and walk through two road tunnels under the New York State Thruway.
- Soon, turn left at the green and yellow "Hiking Trail" sign and climb the hill.
- Bear right at a junction.
- Continue straight (N) through two mowed-grass trail intersections.
- Climb a long, gradual hill to a view of the Rochester skyline.
- Then a long downhill along the edge of the woods.
- Bear right as a small trail heads left.
- Climb steps and turn right along the edge of a yard.
- At the gravel road, turn right and cross the grass to the firehall parking lot.

Date Hiked: _____
Notes:

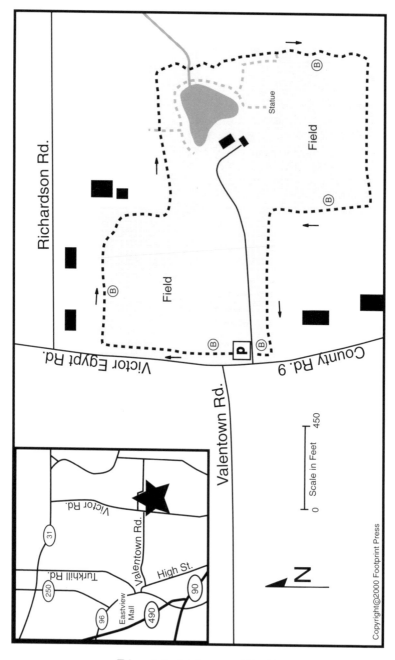

Bluebird Haven Trail

27.
Bluebird Haven Trail

Location:	235 Victor Egypt Road (County Road 9), Victor
Directions:	From Route 96 near Eastview Mall, turn east on High Street and east on Valentown Road. Turn south onto Victor Egypt Road and pull into driveway #235 near the yellow and green Victor Hiking Trails sign. Park on shoulder without blocking the driveway.

Alternative Parking: None
Hiking Time: 45 minutes
Length: 1.1 mile loop
Difficulty: 👣 👣

Surface: Mowed meadow and woods path
Trail Markings: Blue blazes on wooden stakes and blue VHT markers
Uses: 🚶 🎿

Dogs: Pets are NOT allowed
Admission: Free
Contact: Victor Hiking Trails
85 East Main Street, Victor, NY 14564-1397
(716) 234-8226
http://www.ggw.org/freenet/v/vht/

Welcome to the multipurpose nature preserve known as the Maryfrances Bluebird Haven. This land was donated to the town of Victor in November 1996 by Robert Butler in memory of his wife, Maryfrances. The master plan calls for development of the land as a bluebird sanctuary through appropriate plantings and maintenance of bluebird houses. An angel statue was added to the property at its dedication in June 1997.

Mr. Butler still lives in the bright blue house on the property and acts as caretaker. The town of Victor and Victor Hiking Trails with the help of various scout groups will be developing the property by adding plantings and maintaining the trail. The trail circumnavigates the property on a mowed path through meadow and forest. Please follow the blue markers carefully and stay on the trail. Enjoy a quiet stroll on this forever-wild land without disturbing the nest boxes in the meadow areas. On a December afternoon hike we flushed a hawk and an owl from their perches as we hiked this trail.

Eastern bluebirds are in danger because they are cavity-nesting birds. The dead trees and wooden fence posts that once provided homes are rapidly

119

disappearing as we convert our forests and farmlands to housing developments. Other species such as the house sparrows and starlings compete with the bluebird for the few remaining cavities. In many areas of the country, bluebird trails are being created to encourage bluebird survival. These consist of nesting boxes spaced at least 100 yards apart in fields and mowed-grass areas.

The Maryfrances Bluebird Haven is a bluebird habitat developed in support of the bluebird survival effort. There were four breeding pairs of bluebirds here during the 1999 breeding season. Since this nature preserve is a work-in-progress, the Victor Town Clerk's office will gratefully accept contributions toward its enhancement.

Trail Directions
- From the driveway, follow the blue-blazed posts left (N).
- At 0.1 mile, turn right (E).
- The trail bends right (S) along a wooden fence line at 0.2 mile.
- Turn left (W) at 0.3 mile.
- Head toward the grove of pine trees.
- Enter the woods.
- Cross a path to the right, leading to the pond. Continue straight (NE).
- At 0.4 mile the trail bends right (S).
- Cross the pond overflow creek.
- Continue winding through the woods, following blue blazes.
- At 0.7 mile, exit the woods and bear left to follow the blue-blazed posts around the edge of the field (W). In the field far to your right you can see the statue.
- Pass through a hedge row and continue straight (W) at 0.8 mile.
- At 0.85 mile, the trail bends right (NE).
- At 1.0 mile, the trail bends left (NW).
- At 1.1 miles, the trail bends right (NW). Follow the trail parallel to Victor Egypt Road to return to the driveway.

Date Hiked: _____

Notes:

Powder Mills Park

Set in steep, wooded hills, Powder Mills Park offers downhill skiing in the winter and fishing in Irondequoit Creek in the summer. The fish hatchery is also a favorite summertime attraction.

Development of the area began in 1850 when Daniel C. Rand arrived from Middletown, CT, where he worked as a manufacturer of blasting powder.

Rand came to this area and chose a small, ideal spot, far enough from settlements, but still close to the Erie Canal. In 1852 Rand opened his mill for making blasting powder in partnership with Mortimer Wadhams, and called it the Rand & Wadhams Powder Company.

The process for making blasting powder, which is simply a course version of gun powder, had been known for 100 years and involves grinding and mixing saltpeter (potassium nitrate), sulfur, and charcoal. To be an effective explosive, the ingredients have to be ground to an extremely fine consistency.

Irondequoit Creek was dammed to create a pond and a millrace for power to turn the great grinding stones and other machines used to pulverize the ingredients of blasting power. But it was a dangerous job. While in Connecticut, Rand had witnessed several accidents and his attention was drawn to the Rochester area by news of explosions that destroyed some powder mills in Allens Creek.

During construction of his new mill, Rand took several measures to help prevent or lessen the consequences of possible explosions. First each step of the process was performed in a separate building so an explosion in one would not send the whole business up in flames.

Rand also sought to eliminate sparks caused by metal touching metal. The buildings were connected by a narrow-gage railroad with wooden rails on which rode small cars with wooden wheels. And employees were not allowed to have any metal in their clothing. Many men even wore felt-soled slippers because their regular boots were constructed with nails.

Finally, to lessen the chance of fires or vandalism, Rand kept the property off limits to all hunting, fishing, and camping. This created the air of mystery about the area that lingered years after the mills were gone. In the 58 years of operation, several small explosions and two injuries occurred at the mill, but no catastrophic explosions or deaths.

Rand bought saltpeter and sulfur, but made his own charcoal out of willow trees that grew abundantly in the valley. Over the years Rand planted hundreds of new willows to replace those he cut. The willow was burned very slowly to produce charcoal. The charcoal and sulfur were ground together, with the saltpeter being ground separately. After both were

121

reduced to course grain, they were combined and ground together for several hours. They were then formed into large cakes under 3,000 to 4,000 pounds pressure. The cakes in turn were re-ground with graphite, which made the powder flow better. The powder was then sieved to different grades and packed in 25-pound kegs, with the finest being the most powerful blasting powder.

Rand died in 1883 and his partner passed on 3 years later. Rand's two sons, Mortimer and Samuel, continued the mill operation under the name D.C. Rand Powder Co. The brothers quit the business in 1910 and moved to Uniontown, PA, to set up another mill closer to the coal mines that consumed the powder.

The property and buildings were left vacant until 1929 when 290 acres were purchased by the Monroe County Parks Commission. At that time the mill and homestead were razed.

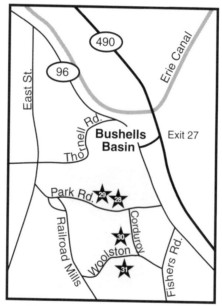

Trails in Powder Mills Park

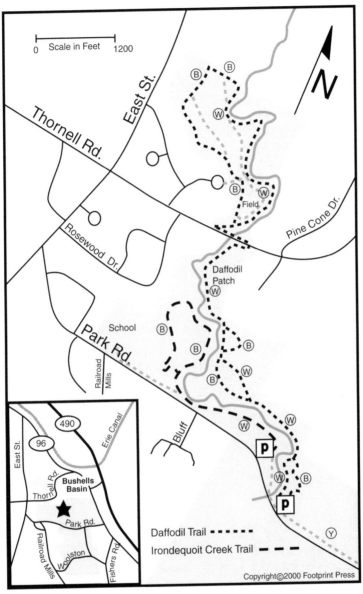

Daffodil Trail & Irondequoit Creek Trail

28.
Daffodil Trail

Location:	Powder Mills Park, Bushnells Basin
Directions:	From Route 96 south of Bushnells Basin, turn west on Park Road. The parking area is on the east side of Irondequoit Creek where the creek flows under Park Road.
Alternate Parking:	On the shoulder of Thornell Road near Irondequoit Creek.
Hiking Time:	1.5 hours
Length:	3.4 mile loop
Difficulty:	
Surface:	Dirt path
Trail Markings:	White and blue blazes
Uses:	
Dogs:	OK on leash
Admission:	Free
Contact:	Pittsford Parks & Recreation 35 Lincoln Avenue, Pittsford, NY 14534 (716) 248-6280 Monroe County Parks Department 171 Reservoir Avenue, Rochester, NY 14620 (716) 256-4950

The Daffodil Trail is a joy to hike any time of year. It follows the contours of Irondequoit Creek as it winds its way through a valley. On the way the trail passes through woods and fields. It wanders near swamps and cliffs with houses perched on the edges, overlooking the Irondequoit Creek valley.

But by far, the best time of year to visit this trail is late April or early May when the daffodils are in bloom. The Pittsford Garden Club planted approximately 2,000 King Alfred daffodils in a shaded meadow along the trail. With the natural music from Irondequoit Creek flowing near, you can sit on a bench and soak in the beauty of a field of yellow blossoms.

You will be following a white-blazed trail on your way out and return on a combination of blue and white-blazed trails.

Trail Directions

- From the parking area, pass a yellow metal gate and follow white blazes through a mowed-grass area. (The blue-blazed trail labeled "Daffodil Meadow" will be part of your return loop.)
- Cross a small wooden bridge.
- Bear right at the junction of the blue trail.
- Pass another blue trail and head uphill into a beech forest, still following the white blazes.
- Pass a blue trail on the right.
- At 0.7 mile, reach the daffodil meadow and a bench for rest and reflection.
- As you approach Thornell Road the trail will bend right and climb the hill to road level.
- At 1.0 mile, cross Thornell Road, turn left, and walk along the shoulder of the road across the Irondequoit Creek bridge. (You may be tempted to use the paved walkway on the south side of Thornell Road but crossing Thornell Road further west puts you just below the crest of a hill. Cars appear rapidly and make crossing more dangerous.)
- When the guardrail ends, turn right and head downhill on a dirt path.
- Bear right to stay on the white-blazed trail at the bottom of the hill.
- Follow the bank of Irondequoit Creek.
- At a "T," turn right.
- At the next intersection, turn right, heading back into woods.
- Continue following the creek and white blazes.
- At 1.6 miles reach a "T" and turn right.
- Pass a trail to the left.
- At 1.8 miles white blazes end and blue blazes begin signalling the start of the return trip. The trail now leaves the creek. From here to the parking area, select the blue trail, whenever you have a choice.
- Pass a trail to the left in a short distance.
- At a wide grass area bear left (S). A farm field is to the right.
- At a "Y'" bear right (S), following blue blazes.
- Pass some small trails to the right.
- At 2.2 miles reach a field and turn right (SE). Head uphill.
- At the top of the hill, continue straight past a trail to the right and a trail to the left.
- Bear right past a trail to the left.
- Bear right again and climb the hill to Thornell Road.
- At 2.4 miles, turn left (E) and follow the shoulder of Thornell Road to the end of the guardrail.
- Cross Thornell Road and head downhill to the creek.
- Bear left and follow white blazes.
- At 2.7 miles, pass through Daffodil Meadow.
- Watch for blue blazes and turn left (E) at 2.8 miles.

The daffodils bloom in late March.

- At a "T," turn left returning to white-blazed trail.
- At a "Y," bear right on blue again.
- At a "T," turn right onto white.
- At a "Y," bear left on the white trail.
- Cross a small wooden bridge and immediately turn left on the blue-blazed trail.
- Follow this blue trail back to the parking area.

Date Hiked: _____
Notes:

126

29.
Irondequoit Creek Trail

Location:	Powder Mills Park, Bushnells Basin
Directions:	From Route 96 south of Bushnells Basin, turn west on Park Road. The "West Area" parking area is on the west side of Irondequoit Creek where the creek flows under Park Road.

Alternate Parking: None
Hiking Time: 30 minutes
Length: 1.1 mile loop
Difficulty: 🥾🥾

Surface: Dirt path
Trail Markings: White and blue blazes
Uses: 🚶🎿

Dogs: OK on leash
Admission: Free
Contact: Monroe County Parks Department
171 Reservoir Avenue, Rochester, NY 14620
(716) 256-4950

The Irondequoit Creek Trail follows the southern shore of Irondequoit Creek then wanders in a loop through a forest in the Irondequoit Creek valley.

Trail Directions
- From the "West Area" parking area cross the mowed-grass area with Irondequoit Creek on your right and the West Shelter on your left.
- Enter the woods near the creek and follow white blazes.
- The trail will swing back near Park Road.
- Bear right to stay near the creek.

A blaze on the tree marks the trail.

127

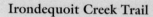

- At 0.3 mile you'll see blue blazes. Bear right to stay near the creek.
- Cross a narrow field.
- At 0.6 miles be alert for the double blazes which tell you the trail doubles back, away from the creek.
- Pass a rusted old plow and disc beside the trail.
- Follow the blue blazes carefully as they snake through the woods.
- At 0.8 mile emerge to a mowed-grass field.
- Turn right and follow the creek back to the parking area.

Date Hiked: _____

Notes:

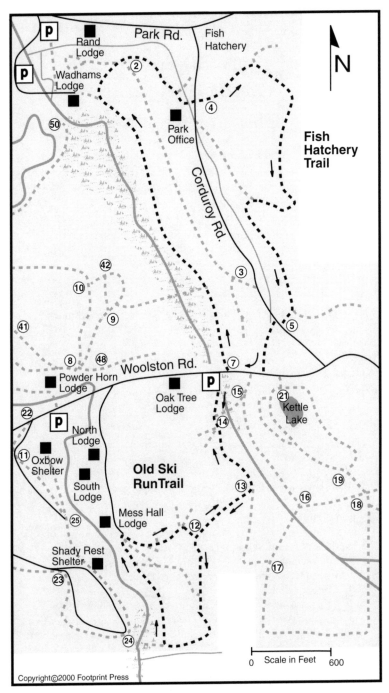

Old Ski Run Trail & Fish Hatchery Trail

30.
Fish Hatchery Trail

Location:	Powder Mills Park, Bushnells Basin
Directions:	From Interstate 490, exit at Bushnells Basin. Turn left on Route 96 (S), right on Park Road, left on Corduroy Road, and right on Woolston Road. Park in the gravel parking lot on the south side of Woolston Road before Oak Tree Shelter.

Alternative Parking: Wadham Lodge or the fish hatchery

Hiking Time:	45 minutes
Length:	1.4 mile loop
Difficulty:	👣 👣 👣
Surface:	Dirt path
Trail Markings:	Blue and white metal signs on trees at trail junctions
Uses:	🚶 🎿
Dogs:	OK on leash
Admission:	Free
Contact:	Monroe County Parks Department 171 Reservoir Avenue, Rochester, NY 14620 (716) 256-4950

This trail begins along the edge of a swamp then climbs an esker. It then dips back down to cross Corduroy Road and climbs through a pine forest. Along the way, you have the option of taking two short side trails. One visits an old mill wheel. The other takes you to the fish hatchery.

Trail Directions

- Cross Woolston Road. Pass through a wooden fence to junction marker #7 and the "Easiest" ski sign. Enter woods.
- Continue straight (N) past a trail to the left, then a trail to the right.
- At a wide junction, marked with a "More Difficult" ski sign, turn right (NE) and go uphill.
  Side Trip to Mill Wheel (0.1 mile): Continue straight (W) from the wide junction. Go past Wadhams Shelter and cross the creek. The mill wheel is in a fenced-in area on the right. Return to the wide junction.
- At the top of the hill bear right. (To the left is a small side loop trail.)
- At 0.5 mile, continue straight (E) through junction marker #2.
  Side Trip to Fish Hatchery: Near the bottom of the hill is a trail to the left leading across the road to the fish hatchery.

- Proceed to the parking lot of the yellow park office building. Turn left and cross the bridge.
- At 0.7 mile, cross Corduroy Road and proceed straight ahead to junction marker #4 and a "Most Difficult" ski sign.
- Enter woods and start uphill through a pine forest.
- Reach a "T," at 0.8 mile and turn right (S). The trail now weaves through the woods.
- Watch for an extreme sharp left turn as you head downhill at 1.1 miles. (If you miss this turn you'll end up at the road near the yellow park office building again.)
- The trail levels out at the base of the hill.
- At a "T" junction turn right (W).
- At junction marker #5 cross Corduroy Road and turn right (NW).
- After 30 feet reenter the woods on the left. This trail junction can be hard to see.
- At Woolston Road turn right (W) and follow the road back to the parking lot.

Date Hiked: _____

Notes:

31.
Old Ski Run Trail

Location:	Powder Mills Park, Bushnells Basin
Directions:	From Interstate 490, exit at Bushnells Basin. Turn left on Route 96 (S), right on Park Road, left on Corduroy Road, and right on Woolston Road. Park in the gravel parking lot on the south side of Woolston Road before Oak Tree Shelter.

Alternative Parking: None
Hiking Time: 45 minutes
Length: 1.4 mile loop
Difficulty: 🥾 🥾 🥾 🥾

Surface: Dirt path
Trail Markings: Blue and white metal signs on trees at trail junctions
Uses: 🚶 🎿

Dogs: OK on leash
Admission: Free
Contact: Monroe County Parks Department
171 Reservoir Avenue, Rochester, NY 14620
(716) 256-4950

You'll climb a hill which once was an active ski hill. Remains of the old lift towers can still be seen. The hill is still active in the winter for skiing and sledding but no lifts operate to take you up the hill. The trail described below climbs to the top of the ski hill, then winds back through the woods to overlook a deep ravine. The return loop passes by Irondequoit Creek.

Trail Directions
- At the south corner of the parking lot, cross through a wooden fence at the sign "No Bikes on Trails."
- At junction marker #14 continue straight (S) and climb a hill.
- Keep left at the grassy bowl area (old ski area).
- At junction marker #13 bear right (W) and head uphill.
- Reach junction marker #12 at 0.4 mile. Turn left (SW) to a gradual uphill.
- Pass a trail to the right. Bear left (SW).
- At 0.6 mile, the trail bends right. A ravine is on your left.

- The trail continues bending right then a trail enters from the left. Bear right (N).
- Pass through a patch of horsetails.
- At 0.9 mile, Irondequoit Creek will appear on your left.
- Bear left to stay on the lower trail heading north.
- Pass a trail to the left that leads to the creek.
- At 1.0 mile, turn right (E) at the yellow vehicle barricade and continue on a gradual uphill. (Straight ahead goes to brown park buildings.)
- Continue straight (E) past a small trail to the right.
- Pass a small trail to the left.
- Emerge to a wide field area (the old ski hill). At each trail junction bear right, staying above the bowl, until you reach junction marker #12.
- Turn left (E) and head downhill.
- Bear left (NE) at junction marker #13. You've come 1.2 miles.
- At the bottom of the bowl, continue downhill.
- At junction marker #14 go straight. (Trail to right crosses a stream.)
- Follow the woodchip path to the parking lot.

Date Hiked: _____

Notes:

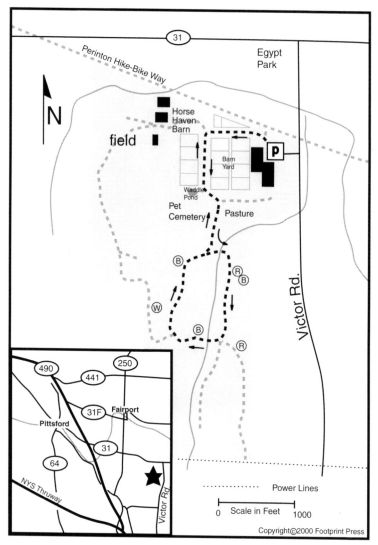

Lollypop Farm Trail

32.
Lollypop Farm Trail

Location:	The Humane Society at Lollypop Farm, Fairport
Directions:	From Interstate 490, head east on Route 31. Turn right (S) on Victor Road and right (W) into the Lollypop Farm parking lot.

Alternative Parking: None

Hiking Time:	45 minutes
Length:	1.3 mile loop
Difficulty:	
Surface:	Gravel, mowed-grass, and dirt paths
Trail Markings:	Within the woods, trails have red and blue paint bands around trees
Uses:	
Dogs:	OK on leash
Admission:	Free
Contact:	Humane Society at Lollypop Farm PO Box 299, 99 Victor Road Fairport, NY 14450 (716) 223-1330 http://www.lollypop.org

Lollypop Farm is the home of the Humane Society of Monroe County. In 1999 it completed a major expansion and moved into new buildings to house stray and abandoned cats and dogs. The main building for animal viewing and adoption is open Monday through Saturday 10 AM to 8 PM and Sundays from 10 AM to 5 PM. The hours may change so call ahead for the latest information.

The trails are open every day from dawn to dusk. From the parking lot you'll walk down a gravel road, passing pens that house horses, fallow deer, ostriches, pigs, llamas, ducks, geese, and an ever changing variety of other animals. After crossing the pet cemetery, you'll enter the woods and complete a shaded loop through the hills in a mixed wood forest.

Trail Directions
- Head to the northwest corner of the parking lot and follow the gravel road, heading away from the main Lollypop Farm building.

- Pass a trail to the right which leads to the Perinton Hike-Bike Way (see page 82 in *Take Your Bike! Family Rides in the Rochester Area.*)
- Continue on the gravel road, between animal pastures.
- At the "T," turn left (S) and continue passing animal pastures.
- After Waddle Pond, the split rail fence will end. Turn right (SE) and cross in front of the pet cemetery, heading toward another split rail fence around a horse pasture.
- Follow the horse pasture split rail fence toward the woods.
- At 0.3 mile, enter the woods on a mowed-grass path. The trail will be marked with red and blue paint bands on the trees.
- At 0.4 mile, turn left (E). (Straight will be part of the return loop.)
- Cross a small log bridge then the trail turns right (S).
- At 0.6 mile, cross another small log bridge.
- Reach an intersection at 0.6 mile. Turn right to head downhill. (The trail now has blue bands on the trees.)
- Head uphill into a pine woods.
- At the top of the hill proceed straight (N), heading downhill. (A hard-to-see trail heads left. It's a white-blazed trail that is passable but not maintained.)
- At 0.9 mile, pass a trail to the right. Continue straight.
- Cross back in front of the pet cemetery and reach the gravel road at 1.1 miles.
- Turn left and follow the gravel road past Waddle Pond and other animal pens.
- At the trail intersection, turn right (E), passing more pens.
- Pass the trail to the Perinton Hike-Bike Way on the left and continue to the parking lot.

Date Hiked: _____

Notes:

Trail Town USA and the
Crescent Trail Association

In 1996, Perinton was named one of the top 10 "Trail Towns" in the United States by the American Hiking Association. The Association recognizes communities that use trails to provide exercise for the body, stimulation of the mind and senses, and a personal connection with the community's natural beauty and past history. The forty miles of trails including Crescent Trail, Erie Canal Heritage Trail (also called the Erie Canalway Trail), and the Perinton Hike-Bike Way achieve this goal within Perinton.

The Crescent Trail Association is a volunteer organization which was organized in 1980 to develop, promote, and maintain public hiking trails in the Town of Perinton. The name originated from the concept of a long, diagonal trail through the town. When viewed on a map, it resembled a crescent moon. Currently, they have over 27 miles of trails passing through woods, marshland, and meadows. The trails converge into the Erie Canal Heritage Trail and an old trolley-bed trail, the Perinton Hike-Bike Way.

Many individual landowners have granted permission for trails to cross their property. The continued use of the trails and the opening of additional sections depend upon hikers respecting the rights of landowners.

- Obey posted signs and respect landowners rights
- No bicycles or motorized vehicles
- No littering, dumping, fires, or camping
- Please protect trees, plants, and crops
- Stay on the trail and hike at your own risk

The Crescent Trail Association welcomes new members. They sponsor a guided hike along a portion of their trails on the second Sunday of each month. Hikes are open to the public. To hear the latest schedule call (716) 234-1621 or check web site www.ggw.org/freenet/c/ctha.

137

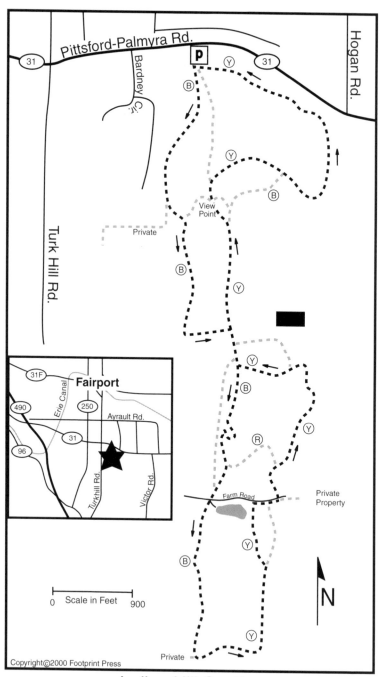

Indian Hill Section

33.
Indian Hill Section

Location:	Route 31, Perinton
Directions:	From Interstate 490, take Route 31 (Pittsford-Palmyra Road) east. Pass Route 250. The parking area will be on the right between Turk Hill Road and Hogan Road.

Alternative Parking: None

Hiking Time:	1 hour
Length:	2.1 mile loop
Difficulty:	👣 👣 👣
Surface:	Dirt and mowed-field paths
Trail Markings:	Orange and blue blazes painted on trees
Uses:	🚶
Dogs:	OK
Admission:	Free
Contact:	The Crescent Trail Association P.O. Box 1354, Fairport, NY 14450 www.ggw.org/freenet/c/ctha

This trail is well-blazed and easy-to-follow. It goes through meadows and woods to a high vantage point (elevation 714 feet) overlooking suburban Perinton and the Rochester skyline in the distance. Follow blue blazes outbound and yellow blazes for the return.

Trail Directions

- From the parking area, head straight (S), uphill, following blue blazes. At the start of the trail you'll quickly pass two trails to the left.
- At 0.2 mile, pass a trail to the right. Continue straight (S).
- At the field, turn right and continue on the blue trail into a narrow woods.
- Exit the woods and cross a field heading south.
- Reach the edge of the field at 0.3 mile. Turn left (E) and head downhill along the edge of the field.
- At a junction turn right (SE) on the yellow trail.
- Pass an unmarked trail to the left.
- Quickly reach a junction of three trails. Continue straight (S) on the trail marked with both white and blue blazes. (To the left is the yellow trail. To the right is an unmarked field trail.).

- Cross a plank bridge at 0.5 mile.
- The trail makes a big S curve.
- Pass a trail to the right. (It leads to the unmarked field trail.)
- At 0.6 mile, pass the red trail to the left. Continue straight (S) on the blue trail.
- The blue trail merges with the unmarked field trail.
- Cross a gravel farm road at 0.6 mile, and continue straight (S) past a pond on your left.
- Follow the blue trail as it bends left at 0.8 mile.
- Cross a small creek on a culvert.
- As you emerge into a mowed field, watch for a sign saying "Stop — end of Crescent Trail." Turn left (N) onto the yellow trail and walk along the edge of a field.
- At 1.0 mile, watch carefully as the yellow trail bears left (NW) away from the large field.
- The pond appears on your left.
- At the farm road, turn right (E).
- In a short distance, turn left (NE) into the woods. Head downhill on the yellow trail.
- Watch for the trail to turn right (E) at a plank bridge. (The red trail goes straight.)
- The trail turns left and crosses another plank bridge at 1.2 miles.
- Follow the yellow blazes as the trail twists. Climb a steep hill.
- Pass a trail to the left. (It is hard to see from this direction.)
- At the "T," turn right (N) to stay on yellow.
- Pass the unmarked field trail to the left, then a trail to the right. Stay on the well-trodden yellow trail, heading north.
- At the junction with blue, bear right (N) and stay on yellow.
- Follow the edge of a field as you head uphill.
- Carefully follow the yellow blazes. (The trail will turn left, but you could easily make a mistake and continue straight.)
- Emerge into a field and the top of the hill at 1.6 miles. Be sure to pause and enjoy the view.
- Choose the middle trail (N) to stay on yellow.
- Again, follow the yellow blazes carefully; you'll pass a trail to the left.
- At the intersection with the blue trail, continue straight, staying on yellow.
- The trail bends sharply left at 1.9 miles.
- Continue downhill to the parking area.

Date Hiked: _____
Notes:

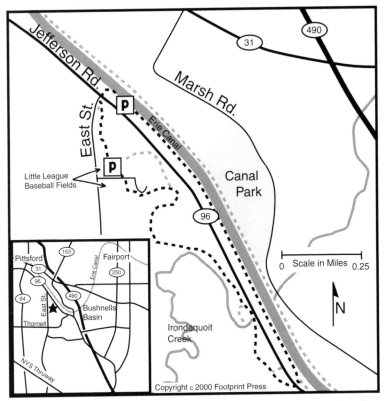

Cartersville - Great Embankment Loop Trail

34.
Cartersville - Great Embankment Loop Trail

Location: Along the Erie Canal, Pittsford
Directions: Park in the Little League parking lot off East Street,
near the corner of Jefferson Road (Route 96)
Alternative Parking: Route 96 near East Street, next to the canal
Hiking Time: 1 hour and 15 minute loop
Length: 2.2 mile loop
Difficulty:

Surface: Mowed-grass and dirt
Trail Markings: White and blue blazes
Uses:

Dogs: OK on leash
Admission: Free
Contact: Pittsford Parks & Recreation
35 Lincoln Avenue, Pittsford, NY 14534
(716) 248-6280

The area you will walk is steeped in history. Once the site of Cartersville, a busy nineteenth century canal port, it had a distillery, warehouses, and a facility for changing the mules and horses that towed the canal boats.

You'll walk on top of the Great Embankment, one of the greatest achievements of the pioneer canal builders. Their challenge was to have the canal span the 70-foot-deep, one-mile-wide Irondequoit Creek Valley. They used earth from the local area to form mounds to join the natural glacial meltwater hills of the Cartersville esker. The great embankment was originally built in 1821-22 and was enlarged several times. It remains today, the longest embankment on the Erie Canal.

Two guard gates, one just west of the trail and one just east of the Interstate 490 bridge at Bushnells Basin, isolate this section of canal in case of leaks or breaks in the embankment, as happened in 1974 when contractor's tunneling under the embankment, inadvertently pierced the waterway. Forty homes were damaged or destroyed as the waters rushed downhill through a 100-foot hole in the bottom of the canal before the gates could be closed. As you cross the embankment, watch for a manhole cover next to the canal. This provides access to a ladder in a shaft leading to the base of the concrete embankment trough, allowing engineers to periodically check the embankment for leaks.

142

The section of Irondequoit Creek that you'll pass was once home to Simon Stone's gristmill and sawmill. Mr. Stone, a Revolutionary War veteran and founder of Pittsford, built his mills in the early 1790s. Milling in this area continued until 1913, when the canal enlargement displaced the mills.

In September 1998 history was once again made at this location. A derecho, or sudden, violent downdraft of air swept through ripping and uprooting the large trees. You'll see evidence littered on the forest floor as you walk this trail. Imagine the power of the derecho (commonly called a microburst) as you hike along.

A portion of the trail follows close to the edge of the Erie Canal; watch small children carefully. Also be aware that poison ivy grows along this trail.

Trail Directions
- From the parking lot, head south over the grass toward the white blaze on a post.
- Follow the blazes around the outside perimeter of a former dump, now grass covered. (Woods will be to your right and a grass hill to your left.)
- Cross over a small culvert onto the dirt town-maintenance road.
- At 0.2 mile, bear right (SE) to head downhill, still following the white blazes.
- A blue-blazed trail enters from the left. It is a shortcut back to the ball fields. Continue following the white-blazed path through the woods.
- At 0.6 mile, Irondequoit Creek appears on the right. Jefferson Road (Route 96) is above you on the left.
- A path veers off to the right. (For a short side venture follow this path down some steps to Irondequoit Creek and a picnic table. The culvert you'll be looking at takes the creek under Route 96 and the canal. It was built in 1916.)
- Continue straight (S) on the white-blazed trail. Wind through the woods.
- Toward the top of a steep hill (at 0.9 mile) is a yellow metal barricade off Route 96. Bear right and continue uphill.
- When you reach Route 96 at 1.0 mile, turn left and cross very carefully. The trail from here follows the south side of the canal. Watch small children carefully. (A right turn connects to the orange-blazed Crescent Trail. The towpath (Erie Canalway Trail) is on the opposite side of the canal.)
- Turn left (N) and follow the mowed-grass path along the edge of the canal. (The canal along this section has high cement walls and banked sides. This is the highest point of the Great Embankment.)
- Pass a wooden rail fence and continue along the canal edge.
- At 1.2 miles, pass the metal "30" sign and the manhole covering the embankment shaft.

- At 1.7 miles, begin crossing through a gravel parking and picnic area between Route 96 and the canal.
- Cross Route 96 when you reach East Street at 1.9 miles.
- Enter the woods immediately behind the East Street road sign (SE corner).
- At 2.0 miles, a blue trail heads off on the right. It's a very short loop to the Cartersville site, which you can take to extend your hike.
- At 2.1 miles, the trail turns left and follows a chain-link fence back to the parking lot.

Date Hiked: _____

Notes:

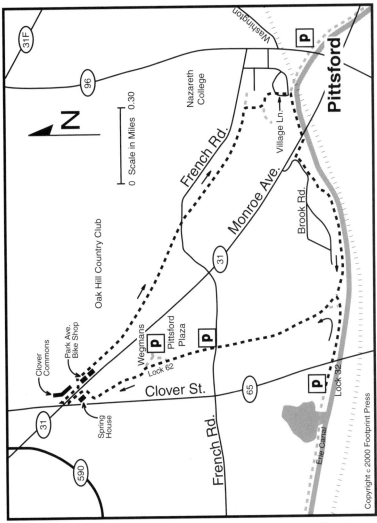

Historic Erie Canal & Railroad Loop Trail

35.
Historic Erie Canal and Railroad Loop Trail

Location: Lock #32 Canal Park, Route 65, Pittsford
Directions: From Rochester, head south on Clover Street (Route
                       65). Just before the canal, turn west into Lock #32
                       Canal Park.
Alternative Parking: At the back of the Wegmans parking lot on Monroe
                       Avenue, Pittsford
                       French Road, between Route 65 and Route 31.
Hiking Time: 3 hours
Length: 5.3 mile loop
Difficulty: 👣 👣
                       👣 👣

Surface: Mowed-grass, dirt, and paved paths
Trail Markings: None
Uses:

Dogs: OK on leash
Admission: Free
Contact: Pittsford Parks and Recreation
                       35 Lincoln Avenue, Pittsford, NY 14534
                       (716) 248-6280

As the name of the trail implies, you will be walking on not one, but two historic transportation paths. The original Erie Canal, known as "Clinton's Ditch," headed north to Rochester. It was opened in 1822, enlarged in the 1850s, and closed in 1920. Mules and horses pulled the canal boats on a towpath next to the canal. You'll walk on some of it, but the rest is now Interstates 590 and 490.

Along the way, you'll see evidence of the Odenbach Shipyard, which made landing craft during World War II, and Lock 62 built in 1855 as part of the first canal expansion. Lock 62 was doubled in 1870 and lengthened in 1887, then abandoned in 1920 when the new canal was routed south of Rochester.

You'll pass the Spring House Restaurant, a lovely federal-style building built in 1829 or 1830 as an Erie Canal inn. At its peak, this area included a resort and spa with a healing sulphur and mineral spring, an amusement pavilion, and bowling alleys. If you have limited time, the 1.7-mile section from Lock 32 to the Spring House is the most scenic and historic.

Then it's on to the Rochester and Auburn rail bed, an active railroad from 1840 through 1960. It was the first railroad east of Rochester and became part of the New York Central system. Both of these sections are maintained by the Pittsford Parks Department. Unfortunately, development along Monroe Avenue in 1999 encroached on the trail. You can still get through but it involves walking along roadways and parking areas behind Cornell's Jewelers and Ride Aid Drug Store. The trail does return to the wooded railbed after the short commercialized section.

The third leg of the trip takes you along the present-day Erie Canal for a scenic walk back to Lock 32 Canal Park. Lock 32 was built in 1912 and still operates today.

Ice Cream: Kilwin's Chocolate & Ice Cream, 3030 Monroe Avenue

Trail Directions
- Begin by heading east on the paved canal towpath past Lock 32. Walk down a flight of stairs. Cross underneath Route 65, where you have a great view of the bottom of the lock.
- After 0.4 mile the path heads slightly inland from the canal. Make a sharp left turn (N) off the paved path onto a mowed-grass path at the map post showing the "Historic Erie Canal & Railroad Loop Trail."
- As you're walking on the 20-foot-wide grass path, notice the remains of the old canal bed on your left.
- The path becomes an old road at 0.9 mile. Remains of the Odenbach Shipyard are on the left.
- Cross French Road and the trail parking area at 1.0 mile. The trail narrows to 6 feet.
- The rear of Pittsford Plaza emerges on your right.
- The access trail down to Wegmans parking is on the right.
- Dual Lock 62 is on your left.
- Follow the trail down steps. (Take the short trail straight ahead to view the second lock.)
- At the base of the stairs, turn right then bear left to cross a small wooden bridge.
- Turn right after the bridge. (Trail to the left goes to homes.)
- Now you're walking in the old canal bed. Trail widens to 10 feet.
- Trail exits at the Spring House Restaurant parking lot at 1.7 miles.
- Head through the parking lot to the sidewalk along Monroe Avenue. Turn left and follow the sidewalk to the intersection of Clover Street.
- Cross Monroe Avenue at 1.8 miles. Be sure to use the crosswalk on this busy street.
- Turn right (E) onto Monroe Avenue along the sidewalk. The trail begins again between Clover Commons and the Park Avenue Bike Shop. This next segment of the trail is on the old Rochester and Auburn railbed.

- The trail passes behind many buildings on Monroe Avenue, including Kilwin's Ice Cream Shop. (Go ahead, you've earned a break!)
- There are some short, rough sections on ballast stone, and you also cross the rear parking lots of some stores.
- The trail returns to a wooded path.
- Cross French Road at 2.9 miles and continue along the railroad bed.
- A cement pillar with a "W" is on the left at 3.2 miles. It alerted the engineer to blow the train whistle.
- At 3.5 miles, pass a cement battery box on the left.
- As you approach a single-story red brick, commercial storage building, take the trail to the right (SE). This intersection has a "Historic Erie Canal & Railroad Loop Trail" sign. You've come 3.7 miles.
- Bear left at the "T" junction at a pine forest. Walk toward a red-brick building.
- Turn right on the paved road and follow it straight to the canal towpath.
- At the canal towpath, turn right (W).
- Walk under the Monroe Avenue bridge at 4.0 miles.
- Follow the canal-trail signs and turn right at the NYS Canal Maintenance property.
- Turn left onto Brook Road.
- Turn left at the yellow metal gate at 4.3 miles, to complete the circle around the NYS Canal Maintenance property. Continue uphill to the towpath along the canal.
- At 4.9 miles, pass the turnoff to the "Historic Erie Canal & Railroad Loop Trail." Continue straight.
- Follow the canal towpath up the stairs to Lock 32 Canal Park.

Date Hiked: _____

Notes:

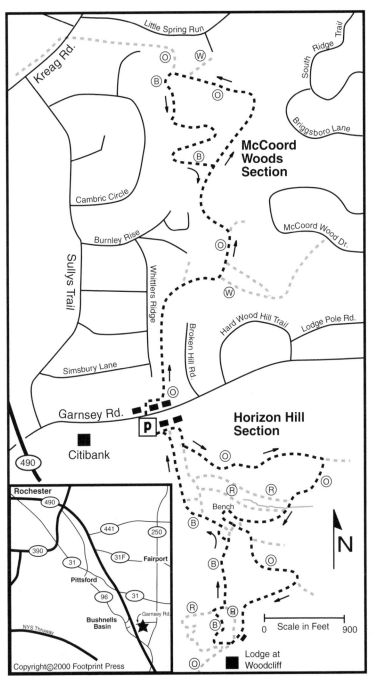

McCoord Woods & Horizon Hill Sections

36.
McCoord Woods Section

Location:	Garnsey Road, Fairport
Directions:	Take the Bushnells Basin exit from Interstate 490. Turn left (S) on Route 96 and left on Garnsey Road. The parking area will be on the right shortly after Citibank.

Alternative Parking: None
Hiking Time: 1.5 hours
Length: 2.8 mile loop
Difficulty:

Surface:	Dirt path
Trail Markings:	Orange and blue blazes painted on trees
Uses:	
Dogs:	OK
Admission:	Free
Contact:	The Crescent Trail Association P.O. Box 1354, Fairport, NY 14450 www.ggw.org/freenet/c/ctha

This well-blazed, easy-to-follow trail begins as a narrow stretch of land between the backyards of private homes but quickly turns to wilderness in terrain sculpted by glaciers. The derecho of September, 1998 felled trees and thinned some sections of this forest trail. According to meteorologist Kevin Williams, "a derecho is a fast-moving, long-lived storm that produces winds in excess of 58 miles per hour over a path at least 280 miles in length. The term was coined by Gustavus Hinrichs, director of the Iowa Weather Service about 1885. He made it up from a Spanish word for "straight ahead," because the debris field from a derecho tends to fall in the same direction."

For a quick escape from civilization and an aerobic workout, this trail can't be beat.

Trail Directions
- From the parking area, cross Garnsey Road and head north on the trail at the "Crescent Trail" sign with an orange marker.
- Bear right to cross a bridge over a small creek.

150

- Follow the orange blazes through backyards where the trail turns left and enters the woods at 0.1 mile.
- Pass a small access trail to the left that leads to houses.
- At 0.4 mile, a small creek appears on your left.
- Turn left (E) on the orange trail (white blaze trail continues straight) and cross a bridge.
- Several small trails lead off; stay on the orange trail.
- Follow switchbacks up a steep hillside at 0.6 mile. Stay on the orange marked trail, don't follow the shortcuts.
- Pass a small trail to the right at the top of the hill.
- At 0.9 mile, bear right on the orange trail as it meets the blue trail.
- The trail heads uphill to the top of an esker (sorry, no view).
- Follow the orange trail down off the esker.
- Pass a small tree-trunk lined trail to the right.
- Stay on the orange trail as you pass the white trail to the right.
- At the blue trail junction leave orange and turn left (SW) on the blue trail.
- Cross a plank bridge at 1.4 miles.
- At the orange trail junction turn right (SW) onto the orange trail.
- Pass a small trail to the left just before the switchbacks. Stay on the orange trail.
- At 2.2 miles, pass an unmarked trail to the left. It leads to the white trail.
- Cross two small wooden bridges then turn right (NW) on the orange trail. (To the left is the white trail.)
- Pass a small access trail to the right which leads to houses.
- Reach the mowed-grass area at 2.7 miles. Turn right and follow the edge of the property until you cross a bridge.
- Turn left then cross Garnsey Road to the parking area.

Date Hiked: _____

Notes:

37.
Horizon Hill Section

Location:	Garnsey Road, Fairport
Directions:	Take the Bushnells Basin exit from Interstate 490. Turn left (S) on Route 96 and left on Garnsey Road. The parking area will be on the right shortly after Citibank.

Alternative Parking: None
Hiking Time: 75 minutes
Length: 2.2 mile loop
Difficulty: 👣 👣 👣 👣

Surface: Dirt path
Trail Markings: Orange and blue blazes painted on trees
Uses:

Dogs: OK
Admission: Free
Contact: The Crescent Trail Association
P.O. Box 1354, Fairport, NY 14450
www.ggw.org/freenet/c/ctha

Hilly terrain on this hike makes it great for a short, strenuous workout. The trail wanders through the glacially sculpted hills in the woods between Garnsey Road and Woodcliff Lodge giving a spectacular view of the Irondequoit Creek Valley and Rochester in the distance. There are many intersecting trails but the main trails are very well marked with colored blazes. Watch carefully for double blazes which signal trail intersections or turns. The loop described follows the orange trail outbound and the blue trail returning.

You may want to use this trail to test your child's blaze-following abilities. Or, as a treat for yourself or your family, hike to Woodcliff Lodge for brunch, then hike back.

Trail Directions
• From the parking area head east on the orange trail.
• Pass two unmarked, mowed paths to the right.
• Continue straight on the orange trail as it crosses a bridge and heads uphill. (A blue trail heads to the right.)
• Cross two more small bridges around mile 0.3.

One of the joys of hiking is finding a scene like this.
A mourning dove and her two babies rest on a rock beside the trail.

- At 0.5 mile, watch for the double orange blazes at the top of a climb; the orange trail turns right.
- Cross a short boardwalk.
- At the "Allan's Walk" sign turn left and cross the bridge. (Straight takes you to the red trail.)
- Another red trail heads to the right just after the bridge. Continue uphill.
- Following the orange trail, turn right at the double blaze and hike along a wide logging road.
- Watch carefully at 0.7 mile as the orange trail veers left off the wide path.
- Turn right (NW) at the next double blaze. (Several unmarked trails lead left. They are shortcuts.)
- Emerge into a clearing with a view of downtown Rochester. There's a bench to sit and savor the view.
- Pass the bench, turn left, and continue on the orange trail.
- Bear left and stay on the orange trail as you climb another hill. (The blue trail heads off to the right.)
- Pass the shortcut trail on the left.
- At 0.9 mile, watch for double blazes and turn right half way up a hill.
- Descend, then ascend again.
- Small trails to the left lead to the Woodcliff golf course fairway.
- The trail bears right at the Woodcliff grounds-keeping area.
- Turn left at the double blaze. (The unmarked trail to the right passes a bench and becomes the red trail.)
- Bear right at the next double blazes. (Left goes to Woodcliff Lodge.)
- Shortly, watch for the blue blazes on the right. Turn right (W) and begin the return leg on the blue trail. (Or you can continue on the orange trail

to the overlook behind Woodcliff Lodge for a wonderful view of the city.)

- At 1.6 miles, follow the blue trail, turning right (E) at the double blaze. (The red trail goes left. You can turn left and loop back on the red trail to add 0.4 mile to your hike.)
- At the "T" junction turn left (W) continuing downhill on the blue trail. (The red trail heads right.)
- Cross a creek at 1.8 miles. The trails straight ahead and to the left are labeled blue. Turn left.
- Reach a "T" and turn left to stay on the blue trail.
- Immediately pass a trail to the right which leads to the bench overlooking Rochester. Continue straight.
- At 1.9 miles, emerge into a field with a view of Citibank below and the Rochester downtown skyline in the distance. Bear left through the field.
- Pass mowed trails to the right. Continue downhill, bearing left until the parking area.

Date Hiked: _____
Notes:

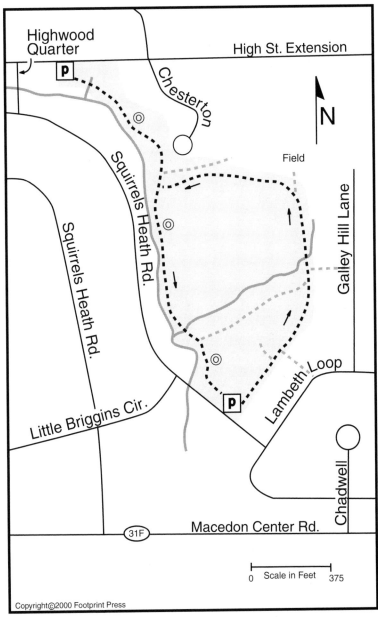

Highwood
Quarter

High St. Extension

Chesterton

N

Field

Squirrels Heath Rd.

Squirrels Heath Rd.

Galley Hill Lane

Lambeth Loop

Little Briggins Cir.

Chadwell

Macedon Center Rd.

31F

| |
| 0   Scale in Feet   375 |

Copyright©2000 Footprint Press

Beechwoods Park Trail

38.
Beechwoods Park Trail

Location:	High Street Extension, Perinton
Directions:	From South Main Street, Fairport, head east on High Street. Continue past Turk Hill Road onto High Street Extension. The parking area for Beechwoods Park will be on the right, past Highwood Quarter.

Alternate Parking: Southern end of the park on Squirrels Heath.

Hiking Time:	45 minutes
Length:	1.2 mile loop
Difficulty:	
Surface:	Dirt path
Trail Markings:	Orange blazes on trees along sections of trail
Uses:	
Dogs:	OK on leash
Admission:	Free
Contact:	Perinton Recreation & Parks Department 1350 Turk Hill Road, Fairport, NY 14450

Beechwoods Park is a 22.8-acre passive greenbelt through a residential area. It is forested with beech, birch, and maple trees. The northern section of trail is a narrow swath through the woods. The southern section has a wide, board-lined trail. The direct route from High Street Extension to Squirrels Heath is orange blazed. It was cleared and blazed by Boy Scout Troop 280. Much of the return loop is unblazed.

Trail Directions

- From the parking area on High Street Extension, head southeast on a gravel path.
- Cross a small wooden bridge.
- Cross a paved walkway and head into the woods.
- Bear left along the edge of a small stream.
- At 0.3 mile, pass a wooden bridge to the right and a trail intersection. Continue straight on the orange-blazed trail.
- Cross a stream bed. The trail will become wide and board-lined.
- Turn left (S) to continue following orange blazes.
- At 0.6 mile, at the parking area on Squirrels Heath, take a sharp left to head back into the woods on an unmarked trail.

- At 0.7 mile the boards lining the trail will end and a paved path will head right to Lambeth Loop. Turn left to follow the narrow woods trail.
- At the "T," turn right. (Left leads back to the orange-blazed trail.)
- Cross a stream bed.
- At a "Y," bear left. Head downhill until you meet the orange-blazed trail.
- Turn right (N) onto the orange-blazed trail and follow it back to the parking area.

Date Hiked: _____

Notes:

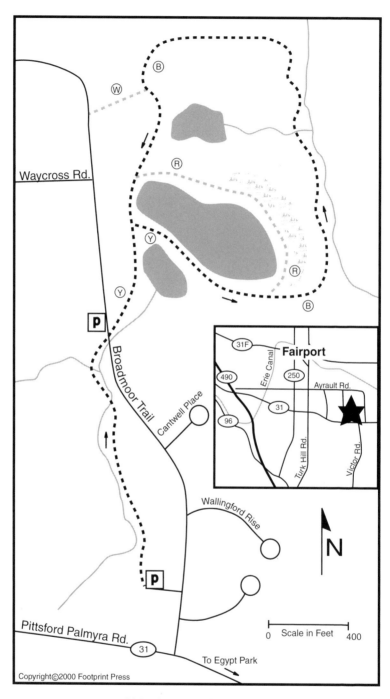

Wetlands Section

39.
Wetlands Section

Location:	Broadmoor Trail, Perinton (off Route 31)
Directions:	From Route 490, head east on Route 31 (Palmyra Road). After Mason Road (shortly before leaving Monroe County) turn north on Broadmoor Trail. Take the first left onto a short dead-end road. Park at the end of the road.

Alternative Parking: Along Broadmoor Road where a small stream passes under the road.

Hiking Time:	50 minutes
Length:	1.6 mile loop
Difficulty:	👣
Surface:	Mowed-grass and dirt paths
Trail Markings:	3-inch Crescent Trail logo signs with trail color indicated in the bottom portion
Uses:	🚶 🎿
Dogs:	OK on leash
Admission:	Free
Contact:	The Crescent Trail Association, Inc.
	P.O. Box 1354, Fairport, NY 14450
	(716) 234-1621
	www.ggw.org/freenet/c/ctha

This trail is a wonderful easy stroll through fields and woods. It passes near streams and ponds with active beaver, and you may notice trees the beaver have eaten. At least two beaver dens are visible, and many beaver trails are in evidence. The ponds are also home to Canada geese and great blue herons. With the combination of ponds, grasslands, and woods, this area is home to many birds, making it a birder's paradise.

Trail Directions
- From the dead-end road, bear right (N) on the trail, heading into the tree line.
- Cross a small wooden bridge.
- The stream will appear to your left.
- At 0.2 mile, cross a second small wooden bridge, then a third.
- At 0.3 mile cross the stream on the forth wooden bridge.

- Cross the fifth wooden bridge.
- Cross Broadmoor Trail. Continue straight (NE) on the yellow trail.
- Pass the first pond on the right. (Houses will be on your left.)
- At 0.5 mile, reach a junction. Turn right (SE) and follow the yellow trail, passing between two ponds.
- At the next junction turn right and cross a wooden bridge.
- Enter the woods and cross three more bridges.
- Cross a boardwalk at 0.9 mile.
- At the next junction turn left (S).
- Emerge from the woods with a pond on your left.
- Continue straight, past the intersecting red trail to your left at 1.1 miles.
- Pass a trail to the left and continue straight (S).
- At 1.3 mile, cross Broadmoor Trail.
- Cross five small wooden bridges as you wind back to the dead-end street parking area.

Date Hiked: _____
Notes:

Northeast
Section

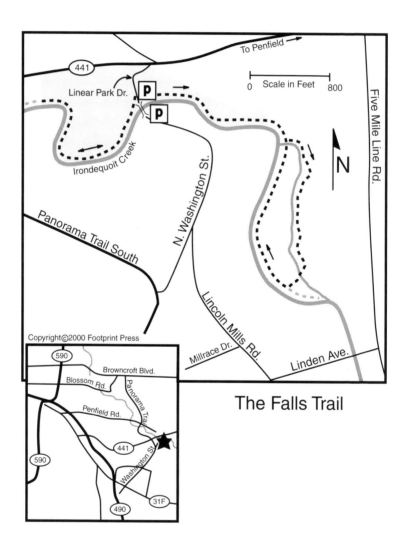

The Falls Trail

40.
The Falls Trail

Location:	Linear Park, Penfield
Directions:	From Route 441 (Penfield Road) turn south on Linear Park Drive. The parking area is at the end of Linear Park Drive.

Alternate Parking: At the end of North Washington Street

Hiking Time:	45 minutes (east route)
	30 minutes (west route)
Length:	1.5 mile loop (east route)
	1.0 mile round trip (west route)
Difficulty:	👣 👣
Surface:	Dirt paths
Trail Markings:	None
Uses:	🚶
Dogs:	OK on leash
Admission:	Free
Contact:	Town of Penfield Parks & Recreation
	1985 Baird Road, Penfield, NY 14526
	(716) 340-8655
	email: recreation@penfield.org

This area of Irondequoit Creek is known as "The Falls" or "The Hollow" because the creek drops 90 feet in one mile, creating a series of cascading waterfalls. The indians called this area SGOH-SA-IS-THAH.

Daniel Penfield settled the area and built the first mill in 1800. It was soon followed by many mills. If you look closely along the creek banks, you'll see some foundations that still remain. The years 1800-1840 were a time of rapid settlement and growth, encouraged by Mr. Penfield's policy of accepting wheat and other farm products for his mills in lieu of mortgage payments until a farmer had enough time to become established.

The businesses built along this section of Irondequoit Creek included flour mills, sawmills, an ashery, an oil mill and soap factory, distilleries, wool and clothing mills, grist mills, a tannery, a blacksmithy, and a slaughter house. Produce from the mills was shipped via Tryon (see Ellison Park on page 176 for more information on Tryon.) to Charlotte, then transported across Lake Ontario to Canada. When the Erie Canal was built it

163

was hauled to the ports at Fairport and Pittsford for shipment to markets in the east.

Two trails are described. One heads east of the pedestrian bridge which spans Irondequoit Creek between Linear Park and North Washington Street. It leads past the cascading waterfalls through the Irondequoit Creek valley then loops back via an island within the creek.

The route west of the parking area winds along the creek edge past towering sand cliffs and ends at the Route 441 bridge. Or, combine the two for a 2.5 mile hike. A three-panel information kiosk was installed at the trailhead in 1998.

One of many cascades along this stretch of Irondequoit Creek.

Trail Directions (east route)

- At the eastern edge of the parking area, look for the "Trail" sign. Walk upstream on the wide dirt path, keeping Irondequoit Creek to your right.
- At 0.3 mile, cross the first of four wooden bridges that span small ravines.
- Reach a "Y" at 0.5 mile and bear left. (Right would take you across a small branch of Irondequoit Creek onto an island. It will be part of your return loop.)
- At 0.7 mile, cross the small branch of Irondequoit Creek.
- At a "T," turn right. (Left dead ends at the end of the island.)
- For the return trip, keep the main channel of Irondequoit Creek to your left.
- At 1.0 mile, cross the small branch of Irondequoit Creek and bear left.
- Cross the small bridges and return to the parking area.

Trail Directions (west route)

- From the parking area, head south with Irondequoit Creek to your left.
- Bear left to stay near the creek on a dirt trail.
- Pass an island in the creek to your left.
- At 0.2 mile the trail bends right at a sharp bend in the creek. Sand cliffs tower overhead across the creek.
- Follow a chipped stone path for a short distance then bear left to stay along the creek.
- Emerge to mowed grass and bear left.
- At 0.3 mile, cross a small wooden bridge.
- At 0.4 mile, cross a second small wooden bridge.
- The trail ends at the Route 441 bridge. Turn around and retrace your steps along the creek edge.

Sand cliffs carved by Irondequoit Creek.

Date Hiked: _____

Notes:

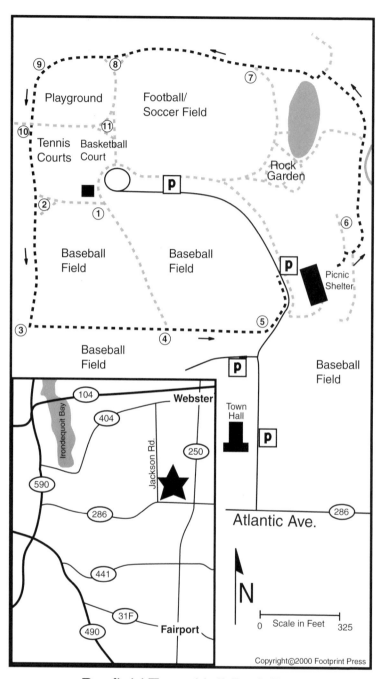

Penfield Town Hall Park Trail

41.
Penfield Town Hall Park Trail

Location: Penfield Town Hall Park, Penfield

Directions: Head east on Browncroft Boulevard (Route 286) until it turns into Atlantic Avenue. Turn north into Penfield Town Hall Park between Jackson Road and Fairport Nine Mile Point Road (Route 250). Pass the town hall building and park just beyond the picnic shelter.

Alternative Parking: The parking area behind the town hall

Hiking Time: 30 minutes

Length: 1.0 mile loop

Difficulty:

Surface: Mowed-grass, dirt, and paved paths

Trail Markings: None

Uses:

Dogs: OK on leash

Admission: Free

Contact: Penfield Trails Committee
Town of Penfield Parks & Recreation
1985 Baird Road, Penfield, NY 14526
(716) 340-8655
email: recreation@penfield.org

Penfield Town Hall Park makes optimum use of the land available. It's home to baseball diamonds, football/soccer fields, picnic facilities, tennis courts, basketball courts, a playground, a fishing pond, a rock garden, physical fitness exercise stations, and a hiking trail. Land acquisition for this park began in 1980. Construction began in 1990 and the park officially opened in 1995.

The trail described here, begins in a wood lot (arboretum), then follows a paved path around the perimeter of the park. Along the way you'll pass portions of the exercise trail. Exercise stations are numbered on the map for Penfield Town Hall Park Trail.

The park contains several paved path loops (part of which are used for this hiking trail) which provide a suitable surface for strollers, wheelchairs, and in-line skates.

Trail Directions
- From the parking area, head south on the paved path.
- At the "T," turn left on the paved path, heading toward the picnic shelter.
- Pass behind the picnic shelter and stonework grill and enter the woods on a mowed-grass path.
- Pass post 34 (wild honeysuckle).
- At the junction, turn right (E) into the woods.
- Pass a trail to the right and head downhill.
- Pass post 35 (mayapple) and post 28 (white ash).
- Cross a small wooden bridge.
- Stay on the main trail. Several small trails branch off.
- At 0.2 mile, reach a "Y." Bear right (N).
- Pass post 24 (poison ivy).
- Reach a "T" at 0.3 mile. Turn left (NW). (Right dead ends.)
- Pass post 13 (douglas fir).
- Reach the paved path and turn right (NW).
- At 0.5 mile, continue straight (W) past 2 branches of a paved path to the left.
- Pass the balance beam exercise station.
- At 0.6 mile, continue straight (S) through an intersection.
- Pass the sit up exercise station and tennis courts.
- Continue straight past 2 branches of a paved path to the left.
- At 0.7 mile, the pavement ends. Turn left (E) and follow the treeline between baseball fields.
- Pass the arm twirl exercise station.
- Cross a paved path.
- At the park road, turn left (E) to return to the parking area.

Date Hiked: _____
Notes:

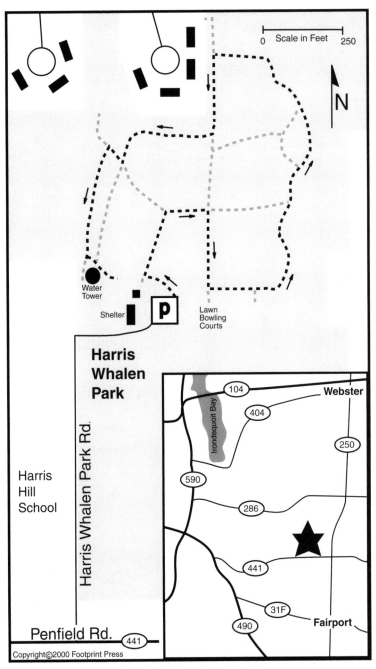

Scale in Feet
0   250

N

Water
Tower
Shelter

P

Lawn
Bowling
Courts

**Harris
Whalen
Park**

Harris Whalen Park Rd.

Harris
Hill
School

Irondequoit Bay

104
404
Webster
250
590
286
441
31F
Fairport
490

Penfield Rd.   441

Harris Whalen Trail

42.
Harris Whalen Trail

Location:	Harris Whalen Park, Penfield
Directions:	Head east from Interstate 490 on Penfield Road (Route 441). Turn north onto Harris Whalen Drive shortly before the Route 250 intersection. Drive up the hill to the parking area to the right of the water tower.

Alternative Parking: None
Hiking Time: 30 minutes
Length: 0.9 mile loop
Difficulty:

Surface:	Dirt and mulched paths
Trail Markings:	None
Uses:	🏃 🚶
Dogs:	OK on leash
Admission:	Free
Contact:	Penfield Trails Committee Town of Penfield Parks & Recreation 1985 Baird Road, Penfield, NY 14526 (716) 340-8655 email: recreation@penfield.org

This trail winds through a stand of mixed forest at the top of Harris Hill. The trails range from 2 to 10-feet wide and are easy-to-follow even though they're not marked or blazed.

Town plans call for additional trails to be built through the western most section of this park.

Trail Directions
- Walk to the northeast corner of the parking area, away from the water tower. Follow the dirt trail into the woods.
- Turn right (N) at the first "T." (Left leads back to a rest room and shelter.)
- At the next "T," turn right (E) and head downhill.
- At 0.1 mile, reach a third "T." Turn right (S) on a wide lane. (Straight ahead is a small trail.)
- Just before the lawn bowling court, turn left (S) onto a narrow trail.
- Cross a cement platform.

- Continue straight (E) past a trail to the right.
- At 0.3 mile, continue straight (NE) past a trail to the left.
- Bear right (E) at the "Y."
- Continue straight (N) past a barely visible trail to the left.
- At 0.5 mile, reach a "T." Turn left (S). (Right dead ends on private property.)
- Head uphill to a "Y." Bear right (W).
- At the next intersection, turn right (W) and head downhill. (For a less strenuous hike, continue straight through this intersection.)
- At the bottom of the hill turn left (SW). (Straight leads to private property.)
- At 0.8 mile, turn left (SE) and head uphill. (Straight goes to the water tower.)
- Continue straight (SE) at the top of the hill, past a trail to the left.
- Emerge from the woods and cross grass to the parking area.

Date Hiked: _____

Notes:

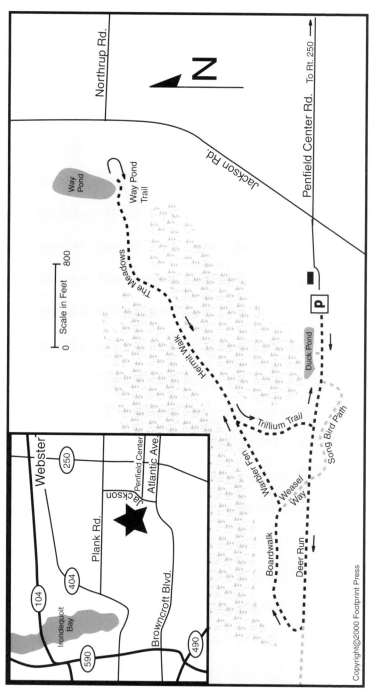

Thousand Acre Swamp Trail

43.
Thousand Acre Swamp Trail

Location:	Jackson Road, Penfield
Directions:	From Jackson Road (between Atlantic Avenue and Plank Road), turn west into Thousand Acre Swamp. Drive into the sanctuary parking area.

Alternative Parking: None

Hiking Time:	1.5 hours
Length:	2.6 mile loop
Difficulty:	
Surface:	Dirt path and boardwalks
Trail Markings:	Wooden signs
Uses:	
Dogs:	Pets are NOT allowed
Admission:	Free
Contact:	The Nature Conservancy
	315 Alexander Street, Rochester, NY 14604
	(716) 546-8030

White trilliums, ferns, and blue violets are among the 500 plant species known to inhabit the Thousand Acre Swamp Sanctuary, along with large hardwood species of northern red oak, white oak, sugar maple, and black cherry. They share the land with deer, rabbit, red and grey fox, muskrat, opossum, mink, eastern coyote, and over one-hundred forty-seven species of birds. It's no wonder that the Central and Western New York Chapter of the Nature Conservancy chose these lands for preservation.

The Thousand Acre Swamp Sanctuary is a great place to watch marsh life. It's easy to spot animal footprints in the mud and get an up-close look at frogs, snapping turtles, and nesting geese. Bring binoculars for the best viewing. Local legend has it that the sanctuary was once the home of a hermit who wanted to get away from the world.

Trails can be muddy and in wet weather, insect repellent is advised. Guided hikes, offered on weekends from April through the end of October, cover a variety of interesting subjects such as wildflowers, coyotes, hidden worlds, and photography. Contact the Nature Conservancy for the latest schedule, or pick one up at the trail head kiosk.

The Nature Conservancy is a non-profit international membership organization committed to global preservation of natural diversity. The Central and Western New York Chapter has protected more than 13,000 acres and owns and manages 29 nature sanctuaries in this region.

The trail described here is an easy walk through forests and swamps. Your feet will stay dry thanks to the many boardwalks.

Canada geese nest at Way Pond in Thousand Acre Swamp each spring.

Trail Directions

- From the parking area, head west across the boardwalk on the Entrance Trail.
- Pass the information kiosk.
- Pass a small trail on the right to Duck Pond.
- Cross another boardwalk.
- Stay on Deer Run and pass the junctions of Song Bird Trail, Trillium Trail, and Weasel Way.
- At 0.4 mile, turn right on Boardwalk Trail to cross the swamp.
- Continue straight onto Warbler Fen.
- At 0.7 mile, bear left on Hermit Walk to wander through the woods.
- At 1.2 miles, turn right (E) on the Meadow Trail and walk the edge of a mowed meadow filled with bluebird houses.
- Turn right (E) onto Way Pond Trail.
- Cross another meadow then enter woods.
- The trail skirts the south end of Way Pond and then dead ends at 1.5 miles. (In spring look for turtles and nesting geese on the island.)
- Turn around and walk back along The Way Pond Trail, The Meadow Trail, and Hermit Walk.
- Turn left onto Trillium Trail at 2.2 miles.
- Reach a "T" and turn left onto Deer Run and follow the Entrance Trail back to the parking area.

Date Hiked: _____

Notes:

Ellison Park

Irondequoit Creek winds through this wooded, hilly, 447-acre park. The first trail takes you to a little used, remote area of the park. The second trail takes you around the historic section of Ellison Park highlighting some of the remnants of the lost city of Tryon.

The lost city of Tryon was the dream of one man, Salmon Tryon. In 1797 he found what he thought was the ideal location for his city. It had everything needed to prosper: waterpower, timberland, a strategic location on land and water routes, a good harbor, and an increasing population.

However, Salmon needed cash within a year and sold it to his brother, John and his partners. They built a business complex consisting of a warehouse, a five-story mercantile, a distillery, a factory for making ash, and a shipping dock with boats. The distillery and ashery were first to be put into operation. Clearing trees then burning them produced potash which was in great demand as an early fertilizer. Sacks of grain were cooked down into liquor in the distillery.

Within the park is Fort Schuyler. The existing fort was erected as a WPA (Work Projects Administration) project in 1938 to commemorate the original colonial trading post that stood in this vicinity in 1721 — 75 years before Tryon was founded. However, the original Fort Schuyler was abandoned after only one year because it became too difficult to keep it supplied from Albany.

Where did Tryon go? Its decline began with John Tryon's death in 1807. In the midst of trying to settle the estate, his executor also died. The stone warehouse and dock were in dire need of repairs. Money was scarce and the property as a whole was impossible to sell. So the distillery was dismantled and individual lots were sold.

In addition to these problems, the War of 1812 added to the decline of commerce on Lake Ontario. Construction of the Erie Canal was the final blow to Tryon. The canal bypassed Irondequoit Bay and provided a safer route without the need to worry about the storms and high winds on the lake.

Ownership changed several times over the years until the twentieth century when residential areas in the town of Brighton sprang up in place of the old farmsteads. Monroe County bought most of what had been Tryon from the Ellison family in 1927 for the creation of Ellison Park.

Note: Three-inch, four-color embroidered patches are available to commemorate your hike. Send $2.75 for each patch to: Troop 55, Covenant United Methodist Church, 1124 Culver Road, Rochester, NY 14609.

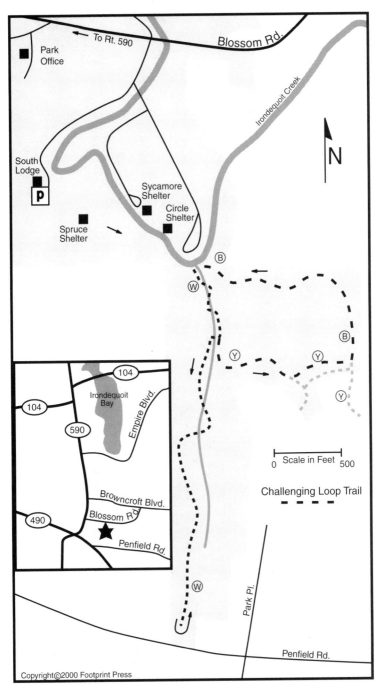

Coyote's Den Trail

44.
Coyote's Den Trail

Location: Ellison Park, Penfield

Directions: Turn south off Blossom Road to the South Lodge parking area

Alternative Parking: None

Hiking Time: 50 minutes (easy round trip)
60 minutes (challenging loop)

Length: 1.7 miles (easy round trip)
2.1 miles (challenging loop)

Difficulty: 🥾🥾 easy trail 🥾🥾🥾🥾 challenging loop

Surface: dirt path

Trail Markings: white, yellow, and blue blazes

Uses: 🚶

Dogs: OK on leash

Admission: Free

Contact: Monroe County Parks Department
171 Reservoir Avenue, Rochester, NY 14620
(716) 256-4950

Coyote's Den Trail leads into an undeveloped, forested area in the southern section of Ellison Park. You'll walk a gradual uphill through the bottom of a ravine beside a small stream, with sharp hills rising all around. Return via the same route for an easy hike or take a yellow-blazed side trail to the top of the surrounding hills for a challenging loop. Many large trees can be found in this area, including a white oak listed in the National Registry of Big Trees.

Eastern coyote, red fox, and deer inhabit this park. If you see canine tracks it's more fun to assume they're from coyote than from the common dog.

Trail Directions

- From the parking area walk southeast toward Spruce Shelter, with Irondequoit Creek to your left.
- Pass young hemlock (evergreen) trees on your right.
- White blazes will lead you along the edge of Irondequoit Creek.
- Turn right just before a small creek. (Across the creek, the blue-blazed trail may be part of your return loop.)
- Cross the creek three times on small wooden bridges.

178

- Caution: At 0.4 mile, watch for the white blazed trail to turn sharply right and cross another small wooden bridge. Turn right and continue following the white-blazed trail. (The yellow-blazed trail straight ahead may be part of your return loop.)
- Stay in the base of the ravine, following the white trail. A few side trails lead to private property.
- At 0.8 mile, reach a grassy opening on Penfield Road. Don't miss looking at the large white oak to your right.
- Turn around and follow the white-blazed trail, retracing your steps.

EASY route
- When you reach the junction with the yellow trail (shortly after the first wooden bridge), turn left to continue on the easy white trail. Follow the white blazes back to the parking lot.

STEEP route
- When you reach the junction with the yellow trail (shortly after the first wooden bridge), turn right (S) for the more strenuous return loop.
- Bear left and climb a steep hill to stay on the yellow-blazed trail. Several unmarked trails lead off to the right.
- At 1.5 miles you'll reach a "T." The yellow blazes will head right and blue blazes will head left. (Turning right on the yellow blazes takes you to a lookout over a Dolomite quarry but ends shortly on private land.) Turn left, following the blue-blazed trail.
- Follow the top of the ridge then head downhill, gradually at first, then very steeply.
- Reach water level and continue straight (NW) along the banks of Irondequoit Creek to the parking area.

Date Hiked: _____
Notes:

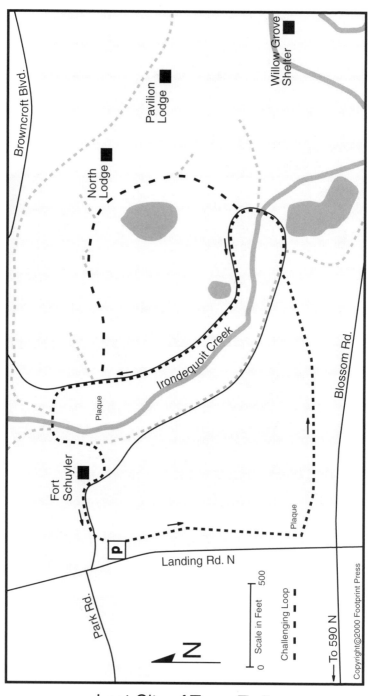

Lost City of Tryon Trail

45.
Lost City of Tryon Trail

Location: Ellison Park, Penfield

Directions: From Blossom Road, head north onto North Landing Road. A parking area will be on the right, on North Landing Road

Alternative Parking: None

Hiking Time: 40 minutes (easy loop)
50 minutes (challenging loop)

Length: 1.4 miles (easy loop)
1.7 miles (challenging loop)

Difficulty: 👣👣 easy loop   👣👣👣👣 challenging loop

Surface: Mowed-grass and paved path

Trail Markings: None

Uses: 🚶 🎿 (ski easy loop only)

Dogs: OK on leash

Admission: Free

Contact: Monroe County Parks Department
171 Reservoir Avenue, Rochester, NY 14620
(716) 256-4950

The 1.4-mile easy loop traverses mowed-grass fields and follows a paved path as it snakes around Irondequoit Creek and passes Fort Schuyler. The more challenging 1.7-mile loop takes a detour to climb a very steep sand cliff to a forested ridge.

Trail Directions

- From the parking area, head right (S) uphill across the grass field toward the corner of North Landing and Blossom Roads.
- Pass an old spring and cattail area on your right. If you look across the road you will see the white "Old Tryon House" built in the late 1700's.
- Proceed uphill toward the corner of North Landing and Blossom Roads to the blue plaque in a prominent rock.
- Continue toward Blossom Road, then bear left, heading downhill, parallel to Blossom Road.
- Continue straight (NE) through a pine forest until you reach a single lane, paved park road.
- Turn right and follow the road across a bridge over Irondequoit Creek. You've come 0.6 mile.

181

- As the paved path bends left, you have a choice. A short easy walk to a plaque in a large boulder or a steep climb around to the same boulder.

EASY route
- Continue following the road as it bears left and follows the creek until you see a large boulder on the left at the end of the mowed area.

STEEP, challenging route
- Take the steep sandy hill on the right up to the crest of a ridge.
- Follow the ridge trail, bearing left at each junction. Keep the swampy pond far below to your left.
- After a steep descent, bear right and pass the Butler's Rangers plaque setting in the ground (sometimes obscured by leaves).
- Continue downhill until you reach an open field.
- Cross the field and a park road, heading toward the boulder

BOTH trails meet here.
- Facing the plaque in the boulder, head to the right (N) and cross the footbridge over Irondequoit Creek.
- Bear left, then after 50 yards turn right and head uphill. Fort Schuyler will be at the top of the hill, to the right.
- Continue uphill until you meet a paved park road. Follow the paved road to the right then take the paved path off the left back to the parking area.

Date Hiked: _____
Notes:

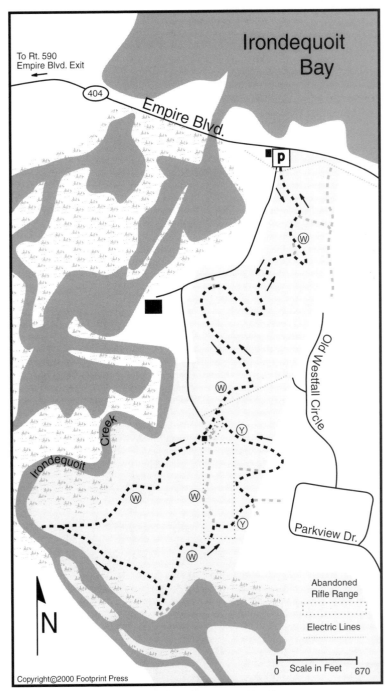

To Rt. 590
Empire Blvd. Exit

404

Empire Blvd.

Irondequoit
Bay

P

W

Old Westfall Circle

Creek

Irondequoit

W

W

Y

W

W

Y

Parkview Dr.

N

Abandoned
Rifle Range

Electric Lines

0   Scale in Feet   670

Copyright©2000 Footprint Press

Old Rifle Range Trail

46.
Old Rifle Range Trail

Location:	Empire Boulevard (Route 404), Penfield
Directions:	Head east from Interstate 590 on Empire Boulevard into the dugway at the south end of Irondequoit Bay. Park behind the C.C. Riders Roadhouse restaurant (formerly T-Bones) at 1129 Empire Boulevard.

Alternative Parking: None
Hiking Time: 2 hour loop
Length: 3.4 mile loop
Difficulty: 👣 👣 👣 👣

Surface: Dirt trail
Trail Markings: White and yellow blazes on part of trail
Uses: 🚶

Dogs: OK
Admission: Free
Contact: Monroe County Parks Department
                    171 Reservoir Avenue, Rochester, NY 14620
                    (716) 256-4950

This is a heavily wooded and a steep terrain area making it a gem to hike. Not only for the wonderful setting, but for its unusual history. Beginning in 1933, this area was home to an elegant, gated gun club consisting of a large 2 story Georgian style clubhouse with a gazebo. The ranges were used by members and also by the N.Y. State Police, Rochester Police Dept. and the N.Y. National Guard.

Within the steep hills were several ranges for rifle, pistol, shot gun and machine gun practice. In 1994 the property was purchased by Monroe County and became the responsibility of Ellison Park. If you look carefully you can still   find some of the target mechanisms and safety trenches. Several sets of cement steps once led shooters to the front of the range. Unfortunately, the clubhouse is long gone, but the gazebo remains, sitting atop a small hill that offered a good overall view of the ranges.

You're in for a challenging but beautiful hike. The trail winds up and down sharp hills and in and out gullies as it weaves through a maturing mixed wood forest. Giant tulip trees tower overhead with lush greenery on the forest floor below, including large patches of ferns and abundant poison ivy. In late spring the creek banks are awash in patches of yellow iris.

184

The rifle range and elegant clubhouse, circa 1930s.
(Photo curtesy of Joseph Schuler)

Trail Directions

- From the parking area, walk south toward a group of three large telephone poles on a narrow, unmarked trail uphill through a field. As you start on the trail a private driveway with lots of no trespassing signs will be to your right.
- Enter the woods in 0.1 mile and pass a small trail to the left. (This small side trail leads uphill to a panoramic view of Irondequoit Bay looking north and to a housing development heading south.) Follow white blazes as you continue straight (S).
- At 0.2 mile, bear left past a shortcut trail to the right. Climb stairs and continue following white blazes.
- Traverse the hillside then make a sharp right turn to traverse the opposite hillside.
- At 0.3 mile, pass the shortcut trail to the right but bear left to stay on the white-blazed trail.
- Head downhill to the valley floor at 0.5 mile.
- Pass a small trail to the right that leads to a private driveway.
- At 0.9 mile, duck under a large downed tree.
- At 1.0 mile pass a yellow-blazed trail to the left. (This will be part of the return loop.) Continue straight (SW) on the white-blazed trail.
- Emerge to a clearing and reach an intersection. (You're now in the old rifle range. To your right is the old road entrance; now private property.) Continue straight (W). The white blazes end.
- Climb a flight of cement stairs and pass under an old gazebo.
- At 1.4 mile, begin descending the hill.

185

Before it spills into Irondequoit Bay, Irondequoit Creek wiggles through a broad wetland lined with cattails.

- Continue straight past a trail to the left.
- At 1.5 miles, reach water level where Irondequoit Creek flows through a man-made dam on its way to Irondequoit Bay.
- Turn around and head back uphill on the same trail.
- Take the first right (SE) to head downhill, following the edge of Irondequoit Creek.
- At 1.8 miles, reach a junction of small trails at a bend in Irondequoit Creek. Turn sharply left (NE) and head uphill.
- Bear right at 2.0 miles. (Left is the lesser used return of the white-blazed trail.)
- At 2.1 miles, reach a junction with a small unblazed trail. Turn left. In a few paces you'll begin to see yellow blazes. (If you miss this turn and continue straight on the wider path you'll dead-end at houses.)
- At 2.3 miles you'll be back in the rifle range area near a cement trough with machinery that used to run the targets and a protective bunker for the target operator.
- Bear right at the trail through the rifle range and climb stairs, following yellow blazes.
- At 2.6 miles, meet the white-blazed trail and turn right (N) to head uphill.
- Pass the trail to the private driveway at 3.1 miles.
- Pass a trail to the right at 3.3 miles, just before reaching the parking area.

Date Hiked: _____
Notes:

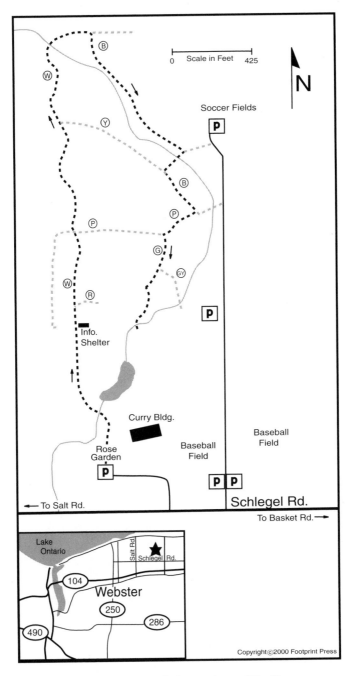

Webster Arboretum Trail

47.
Webster Arboretum

Location:	Kent Park on Schlegel Road, Webster
Directions:	From Rochester, take Route 104 east through Webster. Turn north on Salt Road and east on Schlegel Road. The parking area is on the north side of Schlegel Road.

Alternative Parking: Parking at the athletic fields of Kent Park

Hiking Time:	30 minutes
Length:	0.9 mile loop
Difficulty:	
Surface:	Mowed-grass and dirt trail
Trail Markings:	Wooden trail signs with color designations (colored dots)
Uses:	🚶 🎿
Dogs:	OK on leash
Admission:	Free
Contact:	Webster Parks & Recreation Department 985 Ebner Drive, Webster, NY 14580 (716) 872-2911
	Friends of Webster Trails http://www.ggw.org/webstertrails

Webster Arboretum is a 32-acre segment of the 84.5-acre Kent Park. Gardener Elizabeth Sykes and local garden clubs had long envisioned a unique garden of natural beauty, which would draw people for leisure, educational, and cultural activities. Finally, during the 150th year town celebrations, Webster supervisor Adrian Stanton had the arboretum land set aside, and Parks Director Donna Fauth was assigned to develop the park. George Turner, chairman of the Webster Conservation Board recruited Elmer Smith, Mike Kopicki, and Dick Finicchia to work on the arboretum design. Elizabeth's 20-year dream is being brought to reality through private donations coordinated by the Webster Arboretum Association, Inc., a not-for-profit charitable organization.

Upon leaving the parking area, the first thing a visitor notices are the gardens. Volunteers from the five Webster Garden Clubs have built the Smith Rose Garden and a series of perennial gardens. They're designed to attract humming birds, butterflies, and the awe of human visitors with splashes of

The gardens and Curry building at Webster Arboretum.

brilliant color. Next to the gardens sits the Norman R. Curry building with a multi-purpose room and restrooms.

According to Webster's dictionary, an arboretum is a place where many kinds of trees and shrubs are grown for exhibition and study. Beyond the gardens of the Webster Arboretum, a trail leads past a pond, into the trees and shrubs available for your study. The wide trails are marked with color coded signs so you'll be able to wander and enjoy the sights and sounds of nature with peace of mind. Benches are found periodically along the trail, inviting you to sit and savor your surroundings.

The trails are labeled as:
> Red: Old Apple Trail
> Blue: Judge Trail
> Yellow: Bird Trail
> White: Arbor Trail
> Purple: Sumac Trail
> Green: Kodiak Trail
> Grey: Eagle Scout Trail

Trail Directions
- From the parking area, stroll through the rose garden and head straight back (N) toward an information shelter and sign "Arboretum Trails."
- Pass the information shelter and continue straight on the white Arbor Trail.
- Pass the red Old Apple Trail to the right and continue straight. (The trail will be lined by a rail fence. Notice the old apple trees around you.)
- At the intersection the purple Sumac Trail will be to the right and an unmarked trail to the left. Continue straight on the white trail.
- At 0.4 mile the yellow Bird Trail will head off to the right, bear left (NW) staying on the white trail.

- Enter deep woods and the grass trail will turn to dirt.
- At 0.5 mile, cross a small wooden bridge over the creek.
- Bear right (NE) after the bridge.
- Turn right onto the blue Judge Trail (The beige trail straight ahead leads to the playing fields.)
- The trail bed will return to mowed grass.
- Emerge from the woods and you'll see soccer fields to your left. Bear right to re-enter the woods.
- Cross a small wooden bridge at 0.7 mile.
- Just after the bridge you'll reach a "T" with a yellow trail to the right. Turn left (S) on the blue trail.
- Pass through an open shrub area.
- At the next "T," turn right (SW) on the purple Sumac Trail. (Left goes to the playing fields.)
- Pass through a sumac thicket.
- At 0.8 mile, turn left (S) on the green Kodiak Trail. (To the right is the purple trail.)
- Bear right to stay on the green trail at the next junction. (Left is the grey Eagle Scout Trail back to the garden area.)
- Watch carefully for a left turn to stay on the Kodiak Trail. (Straight leads through an old apple orchard on the non-distinct Old Apple Trail.)
- Cross a small wooden bridge.
- Continue straight across mowed grass. The pond will be to your right.
- Cross through the rose garden to return to the parking area.

Date Hiked: _____
Notes:

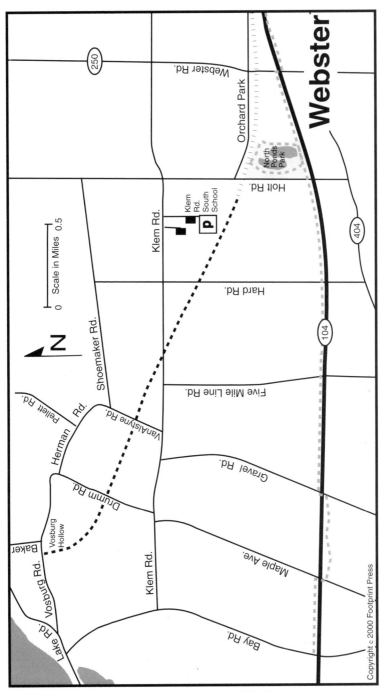

Webster Hojack Trail

48.
Webster Hojack Trail

Location:	Between Vosburg Road and North Ponds Park, Webster
Directions:	From Route 104, head north on Holt Road. Turn west on Klem Road and south into Klem Road South School parking lot.

Alternative Parking: There is room to pull off the road at any of the road intersections.

The trailhead at Vosburg Road is difficult to distinguish. Head west past Baker Road, dip down to cross a creek then head uphill. The trail head is near the top of the hill on the left. It looks like a driveway and has a black mailbox and black newspaper tube marking the entrance. (Note: Do not park in the driveway.)

Hiking Time:	2 hours
Length:	8.2 miles round trip
Difficulty:	
Surface:	Grass and cinder path
Trail Markings:	None
Uses:	
Dogs:	OK
Admission:	Free
Contact:	Friends of Webster Trails, C/O Jack Kerson 1021 Gravel Road, Webster, NY 14580 (716) 671-0258 http://www.ggw.org/webstertrails
	Friends of Webster Trails C/O Webster Parks and Recreation Department 985 Ebner Drive, Webster, NY 14580 (716) 872-7103

This trail is a work in process. The old rail bed has been cleared of rails and ties for 4.1 miles but falls just short of connecting through to Holt Road and North Ponds Park. When this last section is cleared, it will make a great connection to the trails around North Ponds Park and the Webster-Route 104 Trail. (see *Take Your Bike! Family Rides in the Rochester Area*)

At the north end, the Friends of Webster Trails plan to build hiking and biking trails in the five-acre Vosburg Hollow wildlife area which is adjacent to the Hojack Trail near Vosburg Road. For a short walk, the most scenic section is the 0.9-mile stretch from Drumm Road to Vosburg Road. At first cliffs tower above you, then the trail follows a raised bed high above the surrounding countryside.

In the 1850s the farmers of Webster had three options for shipping their produce to market. They could endure an all-day wagon ride to Rochester, an eight-mile wagon ride to the Erie Canal in Fairport, or meet a schooner at Nine Mile Point on Lake Ontario. All were arduous choices.

The prominent businessmen of Webster worked with representatives from other towns between Lewiston and Oswego to inspire the creation of the Lake Ontario Shore Railroad Company in 1868. In 1876 trains began arriving and departing from the Webster station. The line was sold to the Rome, Watertown and Ogdensburg Railroad and the abbreviations R.W. & O.R.R. became known as "Rotten Wood and Old Rusty Rails."

In 1889 a major crash occurred as a westbound train from the Thousand Islands rammed a train as it boarded passengers bound for Rochester. Many Webster homes became temporary hospitals to care for the injured. This crash brought about the use of automotive brakes on railroads.

The Webster train station became a hub of activity. In the fall, the railroad was hard pressed to supply enough cars to transport all the apples from local orchards. The Basket Factory was built along the tracks and became the largest and most productive basket factory in the world. Companies such as the Webster Canning and Preserving Company (a predecessor to Curtice-Burns), the Basket Factory, John W. Hallauer and Sons Evaporated Fruits, Martin Brothers Lumber Company, Webster Lumber Company, and LeFrois Pickling Factory, all owed their existence to the railroad.

The Lake Ontario Shore Railroad became known as the Hojack Line when a nameless farmer's mule-drawn buckboard stopped halfway across the tracks when a train was coming. The framer shouted "Ho Jack! Ho Jack!" to get his mule to move. The amused trainmen picked up on it and the name stuck.

This rail line, like all others in the area, was doomed by the increase in trucks and automobiles. Thanks to the Friends of Webster Trails it became a hiking and biking trail in 1997. To read more about the history of this rail line and the Hojack Station, check the Friends of Webster Trails web site.

Trail Directions
- From the parking lot of Klem Road South School, walk south, across the ball diamonds, and you will find easy access to the trail.

- Turn right (W) along the 8-foot-wide rail bed. (The trail to the left (E) is not yet cleared to Holt Road.)
- Cross Hard Road at 0.5 mile.
- On your left, watch for the cement pillar with a "W," telling the train's engineer to blow the whistle.
- At 1.4 miles, reach Klem Road. Cross diagonally toward the left.
- Cross VanAlstyne Road at 2.3 miles.
- Pass an old cement railroad post inscribed "P87," denoting 87 miles to Pulaski. Pulaski must have been a major port into Lake Ontario in the heyday of the railroads.
- At 3.2 miles, pass a yellow metal trail barricade and cross Drumm Road diagonally to the left.
- At Vosburg Road, turn around and retrace the path.

Date Hiked: _____
Notes:

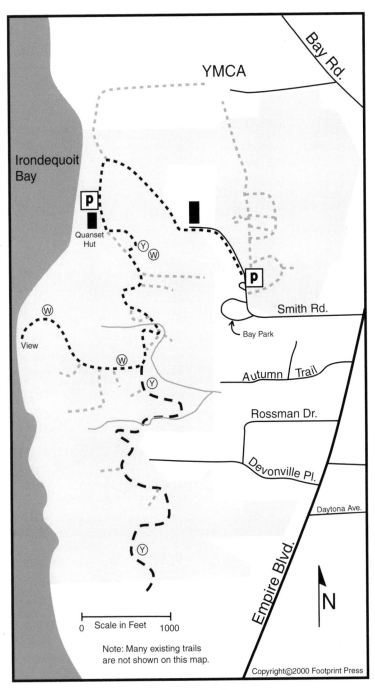

Irondequoit
Bay

YMCA

Bay Rd.

P

Quanset
Hut

Ⓨ Ⓦ

Ⓦ

View

Ⓦ

Ⓨ

P

Smith Rd.

Bay Park

Autumn Trail

Rossman Dr.

Devonville Pl.

Daytona Ave.

Empire Blvd.

Ⓨ

N

0   Scale in Feet   1000

Note: Many existing trails
are not shown on this map.

Copyright©2000 Footprint Press

Bay Trail

195

49.
Bay Trail

Location:	Irondequoit Bay Park East (off Empire Boulevard)
Directions:	From Empire Boulevard turn west onto Smith Road. Park in a grass parking area beside the circle near a yellow metal barricade.

Alternate Parking: If the gates are open you can drive down to water level and park just before the quonset hut.

Hiking Time:	1.5 hours (white-blazed trail)
	1.75 hours (yellow-blazed trail)
Length:	2.4 miles round trip (white-blazed trail)
	3.0 miles round trip (yellow-blazed trail)
Difficulty:	👢 👢 👢 👢
Surface:	dirt trails
Trail Markings:	white and yellow blazes
Uses:	🚶
Dogs:	OK on leash
Admission:	Free
Contact:	Monroe County Parks Department
	171 Reservoir Avenue, Rochester, NY 14620
	(716) 256-4950

Irondequoit Bay Park East is a county park that covers 182 acres of steep, wooded ridges and valleys. There are many large hemlock and oak trees. The park is undeveloped and unknown even to most area residents.

Two possible routes are described here. They begin on the same path and are blazed white and yellow. When they diverge, the white-blazed trail leads west to a promontory at the bay's edge. The white blazes are growing faint with age. The yellow-blazed trail continues deep into the ravines until the blazes stop.

There are many unblazed trails throughout the park. If you decide to fol-low them, take a compass and be careful not to lose your way. Soon each ravine and trail begins to look the same, adding another challenge to the hike! If you're a backpacker, preparing for an Adirondack Mountain hike or perhaps a thru-hike of the Appalachian Trail, this park makes a perfect prac-tice ground. Strap on your pack and wander the steep hills. Your legs and circulatory system will be in shape in no time.

Trail Directions
- From the circle follow the road down the hill (W) past a Town of Penfield building.
- The road will turn to gravel then to dirt as you approach water level.
- At the bottom of the hill, turn left. (The trail to the right goes to the Bay View YMCA.)
- Pass a metal building (quonset hut) used by the YMCA and follow the white and yellow blazes on the trees.
- At the first "Y" go either direction. They converge shortly. (Bearing left is less steep.)
- At the next "Y," bear right and head downhill. (Through this section it's easier to follow the bright yellow blazes.)
- Pass a trail to the right.
- At the bottom of the hill cross a small stream on a wooden bridge.
- The trail will ascend the hill.
- At the "Y" bear right away from the creek. This is quickly followed by another right turn and an uphill climb.
- Continue following the blazes along the ridge.
- At the next "Y" it's decision time. Right is white-blazed and left is yellow-blazed.

White-blazed Trail:
- Bear right and follow the top of a ridge.
- The trail will bend left and head downhill to a promontory overlooking the bay.
- Turn around and retrace your path, following white blazes back to the parking area.

Yellow-blazed Trail:
- Bear left, following yellow blazes.
- Bear left past a trail to the right.
- Pass a trail to the left.
- Wind downhill, following yellow blazes.
- Reach a small stream bed and turn right (W), keeping the stream to your left.
- Cross the stream bed.
- Keep the stream bed to your right for a while then cross over to the other side again.
- Stay in the valley, crossing a trail intersection.
- Cross the stream bed again.
- The trail heads gradually uphill (SW). Blazes are scarce.
- At a "T," turn left (S).
- You'll see yellow blazes near the crest of the hill.
- At a "Y," bear left toward the yellow blaze.
- Head downhill.

- When you see orange paint dots on the trees, it's time to turn around and follow the yellow blazes back to the parking area. (You can create a loop but the many trails in this area are either unblazed or blazed with orange dots. It's very easy to get lost.)

Bonus:

Behind the upper level parking area are more trails that cover a small area on level ground. The main trail leads to the Bay View YMCA, while another goes to the lilac nursery for the Monroe County Department of Parks.

Date Hiked: _____
Notes:

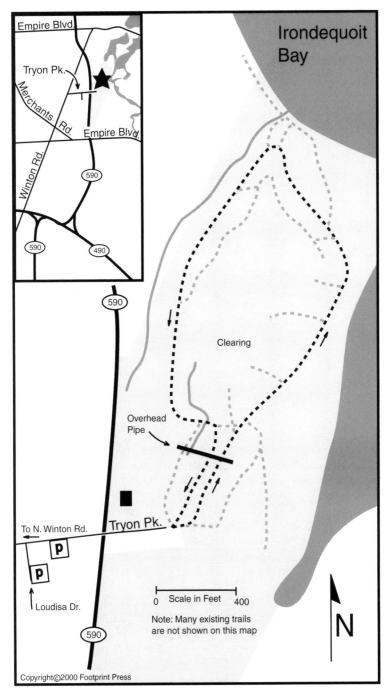

Empire Blvd.

Tryon Pk.

Merchants Rd.

Winton Rd.

Empire Blvd.

590

590   490

Irondequoit
Bay

590

Clearing

Overhead
Pipe

To N. Winton Rd.   Tryon Pk.

P

P

Loudisa Dr.

590

0   Scale in Feet   400

Note: Many existing trails
are not shown on this map

N

Copyright©2000 Footprint Press

Trails of Tryon Park   199

50.
Tryon Park Trail

Location:	Tryon Park, Rochester
Directions:	From North Winton Road turn west onto Tryon Park Road. Park on Tryon Park Road before the Interstate 590 overpass or at the end of Loudisa Drive in the ball field parking area. Do not park between Interstate 590 and the trailhead.
Hiking Time:	45 minutes
Length:	1.2 mile loop
Difficulty:	👣 👣 👣
Surface:	Dirt trails
Trail Markings:	White blazes on trees
Uses:	🚶
Dogs:	OK on leash
Admission:	Free
Contact:	Monroe County Parks Department 171 Reservoir Avenue, Rochester, NY 14620 (716) 256-4950

Tryon Park, dedicated in 1971, is a hilly wooded, 80-acre oasis within a populated city area. It's a delightful walk through mature woods with views of Irondequoit Bay. The noise of Interstate 590 reminds you that civilization isn't far away. The park is on the site of the city's old sewage plant, but all that remains is an above-ground delivery pipe. Try this trail when leaves are off the trees for the best panoramic views of creek waters winding their way through cattail wetlands at the southern end of Irondequoit Bay.

The loop described here is white-blazed. It starts on high ground, dips down to water level, then climbs back to a ridge as it loops back to Tryon Park Road. The adventurous can spend many hours hiking all the trails in this park.

Although bicycling is illegal in this park (as in all Monroe County Parks), you'll see many tracks made by mountain bikes. Take along a small trash bag and pick up litter as you hike. This trail is a litter magnet and needs some TLC (tender loving care) from each person who traverses its hills.

Trees and shrubs are numbered along the trail with three-inch round orange disks. Watch for the numbers and test your tree identification skills.

1. Northern red oak
2. Sugar maple
3. Tulip tree
4. White oak
5. Basswood
6. Flowering dogwood
7. Sassafras
8. White pine
9. Red osier dogwood
10. Buckthorn
11. Cottonwood
12. Pignut hickory
13. Gray birch
14. Black locust
15. Ailanthus
16. Box elder
17. Black oak
18. Shadbush
19. Cherry
20. Blue beech (Ironwood)
21. Hop hornbeam
22. American beech
23. Black cherry
24. Black birch
25. Canadian hemlock

Trail Directions

- At end of Tryon Park Road, pass a yellow barricade and bear left on the old abandoned road. (Another trail heads right over a manhole cover.)
- Pass under the old sewage delivery pipe.
- Carefully follow the white blazes on the trees. There are many intersecting, unblazed trails. The white-blazed trail will leave the old paved road near the lowlands of Irondequoit Bay and head downhill to water level.
- The trail leads to a view of the Irondequoit Creek wetlands area with Irondequoit Bay to the north.
- Continue following the white blazes. They'll lead you uphill to a ridge line with a deep gorge to your right.
- Road noise will increase as the trail comes closer to Interstate 590
- Head downhill and cross a small stream bed.
- At a "T" the white-blazed trail turns right and heads uphill.
- Cross under the sewage pipeline.
- Continue uphill to Tryon Park Road.

Date Hiked: _____

Notes:

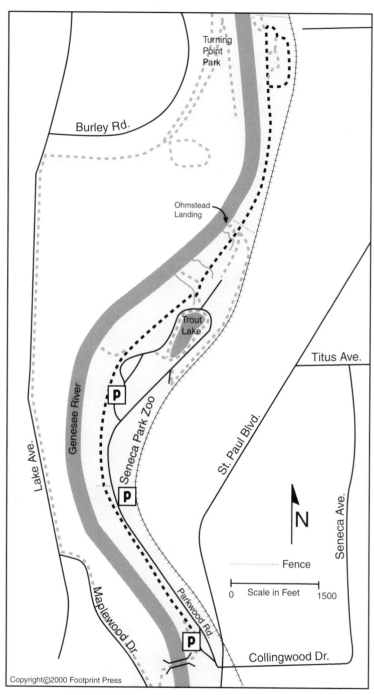

Turning Point Park

Burley Rd.

Ohmstead Landing

Trout Lake

Genesee River

Lake Ave.

Seneca Park Zoo

Titus Ave.

St. Paul Blvd.

Seneca Ave.

N

Maplewood Dr.

Parkwood Rd.

Collingwood Dr.

·········· Fence

Scale in Feet
0   1500

Copyright@2000 Footprint Press

Olmsted/Seneca Trail

51.
Olmsted/Seneca Trail

Location: Seneca Park on Parkwood Road, Rochester

Directions: From Route 104, exit north onto St. Paul Boulevard. Turn east onto Parkwood Road toward the Seneca Park Zoo. Park at the first car turn around after entering the park, near the Monroe County Pure Waters bridge.

Alternative Parking: Several spots along Parkwood Road, in the zoo parking lot, or along the road as it circles Trout Lake.

Hiking Time: 2.5 hours minimum (without side trips into the gorge)

Length: 4.3 miles round trip

Difficulty:

Surface: Woodchip path, gravel path

Trail Markings: None

Uses:

Dogs: OK on leash

Admission: Free

Contact: Monroe County Parks Department
171 Reservoir Avenue, Rochester, NY 14620
(716) 256-4950

The 297-acre Seneca Park was designed by Frederick Law Olmsted who is considered to be the founder of landscape architecture. He was prolific in the Rochester area where he designed four major parks: Seneca, Genesee Valley, Highland, and Maplewood.

Olmsted's designs were revolutionary for the late 1800s. Instead of laying out precise squares and gardens, he planned clumps of woods, meandering trails, bridle paths and spectacular views. He planted trees carefully to effect a "forested" look. This natural, quiet look was half of Olmsted's design philosophy. The other half created spaces for more active use, such as the open areas for ball fields and ponds for swimming in summer and ice skating in winter. Pavilions and bridges were designed in a neo-classic style to separate activity areas.

"A park should be accessible to the poor as well as the rich. It should be the beauty of the fields, the meadows, the prairies of green pastures, and the still waters. What we want to gain is tranquility and rest to the mind."   Frederick Law Olmsted

203

In its days of grandeur, swan boats plied back and forth taking passengers for a ride on Trout Lake. The boats carried 15 to 20 passengers on bench seats while the driver sat on a cast iron seat between two 4 foot high swans and peddled the pontoon boat. Today a paved path and picnic tables encircle the lake. The park is also home to the Seneca Park Zoo.

The Olmsted/Seneca Trail runs parallel to the steep Genesee River gorge. While there are no blazes, the trail is well defined and up to eight feet wide at times. Along the trail are dock access trails leading to the river's edge. Hiking down reveals the 400 million years of geologic history in the gorge walls. On the trail you pass wetlands, a pond, and many beautiful scenic views of the river.

The Monroe County Pure Waters bridge was built in 1988. The 670 foot pedestrian bridge gives an excellent view of the surrounding gorge and river 100 feet below. It connects to the Genesee River Trail #2 (page 24) on the west bank of the river.

Trail Directions
- From the parking area near the Monroe County Pure Waters bridge, head northwest on the wide mulched trail with the Genesee River to your left.
- Pass a ramp entrance to the bridge.
- Pass the zoo parking lot.
- Follow the trail down to the fence opening on the left (at 0.5 mile) which was made to allow hikers only, and skinny ones at that, to pass through.
- Begin an easy descent on the wood chip path. Because the trail is in a park, there are many side trails off to the right. Stay on the main trail always heading north, staying near the river gorge.
- At 0.8 mile, pass the first trail into the gorge on the left.
- Pass restrooms.
- Trout Lake will appear to the right.
- At 1.1 miles, pass your first lookout. This is a nice place to sit at the bench and enjoy the view.
- At the "Y" bear right and cross a small bridge over a stream. (To the left is a small picnic/viewing area.)
- Bear left immediately after the bridge.
- Proceed gradually downhill, crossing two wooden bridges.
- At 1.2 miles, immediately after the second bridge, a trail to the left goes down to a dock on the Genesee River. This is the second side trail you'll have the chance to take, if you want to.
- Pass additional views with benches.
- At 1.4 miles, cross a small creek on a wooden bridge.
- Bear right at the fork, just before the second rise. (The trail to left with a split rail fence leads down 0.1 mile to a river dock and a waterfall view.

This is called Olmsted Landing after Frederick Law Olmsted, the park's designer.)

- The trail now meets a gravel park access road. Follow the road, continuing to bear left (N) through a 10 foot high fence gate at 1.5 miles.
- Follow the old maintenance access road. (This is the narrowest part of the park with the gorge on the left and an abandoned railroad bed and private homes on the right.)
- At 1.8 miles, pass a gated access road on the right used by the park for composting.
- At the top of the next hill, turn right (SE) at the small side trail marked with orange diamond markers. You're heading away from the river gorge.
- Continue straight through a small trail intersection.
- At 2.1 miles, reach a "T," turn right again and bear left past the locked Seneca Road entrance (locked to vehicles, open to pedestrians).
- Follow the trail around to the left leading back to the gorge.
- Reach a four-way intersection at the edge of the gorge. (This is the farthest point north for the trail. Across the gorge is Turning Point Park - Trail #53 (page 209). One of the two trails on the right leads to the river and a dock. The other continues heading north to the end of county property and a gate.) Bear left and begin your return trip heading south along the gorge.
- Follow the edge of the gorge back to the gravel access road.
- At 2.4 miles, turn right (S) and follow the access road until you pass the open fence gate.
- Immediately watch for the trail on the right and turn right to stay near the gorge.
- At this point you will be retracing your steps back to where you began. Remember to stay on the trail nearest the gorge.

Date Hiked: _____

Notes:

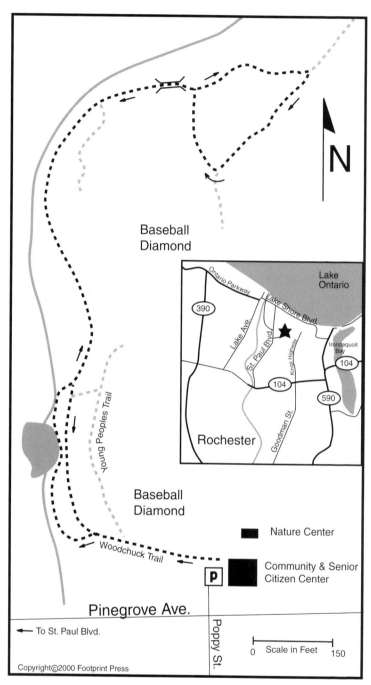

Baseball
Diamond

Ontario Parkway

390

Lake Ave.

St. Paul Blvd.

Lake Shore Blvd

Kings Highway

Lake
Ontario

Irondequoit
Bay

104

104

590

Goodman St.

Rochester

N

Baseball
Diamond

Young Peoples Trail

Nature Center

Community & Senior
Citizen Center

Woodchuck Trail

P

Pinegrove Ave.

← To St. Paul Blvd.

Poppy St.

Scale in Feet
0   150

Copyright©2000 Footprint Press

Helmer Nature Center Trails

52.
Helmer Nature Center Trails

Location:	Pinegrove Avenue, Irondequoit
Directions:	From Route 104, head north on St. Paul Boulevard. Turn east on Pine Grove Avenue. The Helmer Nature Center parking lot will be on the left (N).

Alternative Parking: None
Hiking Time: 45 minutes
Length: 1.2 mile loop
Difficulty: 🥾 🥾 🥾

Surface: Wood chip path
Trail Markings: Some overhead signs
Uses: 🚶

Dogs: Pets are NOT allowed
Admission: Free
Contact: Helmer Nature Center
154 Pinegrove Avenue
Rochester, NY 14617
(716) 336-3035

The Helmer Nature Center began operation in 1973 under the West Irondequoit School District. The center utilizes the natural world as a classroom, providing learning opportunities, encouraging environmental awareness, and fostering the concept of global stewardship. They offer a wide range of educational activities including classes in nature awareness, animal habitats, snowshoeing, Native American culture, pioneer living, outdoor cooking, field studies, etc. After enjoying the trails stop in the nature center to find out about the educational activities and consider becoming a member.

The trail takes you through a hilly forest. This area was formerly comprised of vineyards with terracing which can still be seen on the wooded hillsides. You'll pass a pond and stream and climb a series of stairs. At the northern end of the loop described, a trail continues north through the valley for 0.5 mile before petering out at a stream. It's a very peaceful woods walk and a nice way to extend your hike.

Trail Directions

- From the parking area head left (W) passing behind the baseball diamond fence.
- Continue straight on Woodchuck Trail, under a wooden sign.
- Proceed down steps.
- At a "Y," bear left to continue down more steps.
- At 0.2 mile cross a boardwalk at the edge of a pond.
- Climb some steps.
- At the "T," turn left (N). Notice the abandoned vineyard terraces on the hillsides.
- Reach a "Y," and bear left (N).
- Cross a wooden bridge.
- Continue straight, passing a trail to the right.
- At a "T," turn right staying on the board-lined trail. (The trail to the left wanders through the valley for 0.5 mile before disappearing.)
- At 0.7 miles, turn right on a board-lined trail, just before the "Nature Center" sign.
- Head down stairs.
- At a "T," turn left and cross the wooden bridge.
- Continue straight, passing a trail to the left.
- Continue straight, passing a trail to the right.
- Continue straight, passing a trail to the left.
- Continue straight, passing a trail to the right.
- Climb stairs.
- Go straight, past the "Young Peoples Trail" on the left.
- Pass the baseball diamond and return to the parking area.

Date Hiked: _____
Notes:

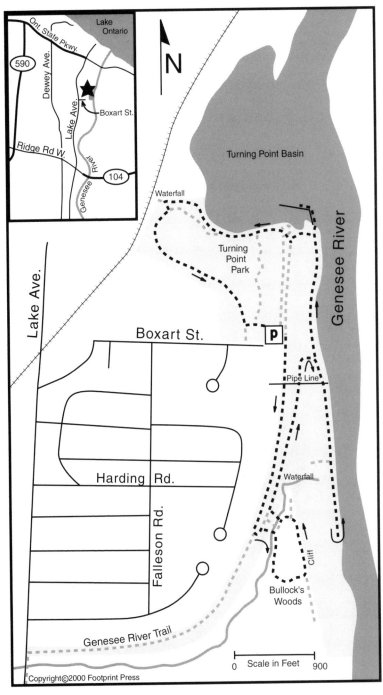

Turning Point Park &
Bullock's Woods Preserve

53.
Turning Point Park & Bullock's Woods Preserve

Location: Boxart Street, Charlotte

Directions: From Lake Avenue (south of Stonewood Road), turn east on Boxart Street. The parking area is at the end of Boxart Street.

Alternative Parking: None

Hiking Time: 2 hour loop

Length: 3.0 mile loop

Difficulty:

Surface: Dirt path, paved trail

Trail Markings: None

Uses: 🥾 ⛷

Dogs: OK on leash

Admission: Free

Contact: Department of Parks, Recreation & Human Services
City of Rochester
400 Dewey Avenue, Rochester, NY 14613
(716) 428-6770

Turning Point Park is a 112-acre wilderness setting in an urban environment. The term "Turning Point" has double meaning to the Charlotte residents nearby. Historically, the wide basin in the nearby Genesee River was a physical place that ships could turn around before encountering the Lower Falls. This was once a heavily used industrial area with ships visiting docks to load and unload coal, wheat, feldspar, paper boxes, and tourists. An active cement plant still operates on this site.

In 1972 the Rochester-Monroe County Port Authority announced plans to build an oil storage tank farm on the site. Area residents, led by Bill Davis fought the plan which would have bulldozed a stand of 200-year-old oak trees and cut off community access to the river. They achieved a "Turning Point" in getting the city to turn away from commercial development of the river waterfront and toward its recreational use. The city bought the land in 1976 and opened Turning Point Park in 1977.

From the parking area, your journey will start high in a cliff with panoramic views of the river valley below. You'll walk a paved path, gradually downhill, then veer off for a loop through Bullock's Woods. Back to an old railroad grade, you'll continue downhill, passing a waterfall, until you reach river level. Walking along the river you'll pass a series of docks, both active and abandoned. Essroc Materials, Inc., Great Lakes Cement Division still uses these docks to unload dry cement to the large storage tanks which sit atop the cliff.

After exploring the river's edge, you'll climb back uphill. Then loop through a forest with 200-year-old oak trees, passing another waterfall, before returning to the parking area. Thanks Bill Davis for having the foresight to save this urban treasure.

Cement gets pumped from cargo ships through green pipes to storage tanks at the top of the cliff in Turning Point Park.

211

The *Essroc* delivers cement to the docks at Turning Point Park for the Essroc Materials Company, Great Lakes Cement Division.

Trail Directions

- From the parking area, walk south on the paved walkway toward the "Turning Point Park" sign and overhead green pipes. This paved section of the trail is part of the Genesee River Trail #2 (page 24).
- Pass under the green pipes. (They pump dry cement from ships at the dock to the large storage tanks.)
- At 0.3 mile, take a sharp left off the abandoned railbed, and double back on a dirt trail just before some wooden posts.
- Take the first right and head downhill on a small trail. (If you miss this, there are two more trails to the right that head downhill. Any of them will take you across a small creek.)
- Cross the small creek.
- Immediately, turn right (S), following a trail marked with red wooden squares on the trees.
- The trail circles left to a cliff overlooking the river. At 0.5 mile, turn left (N) to follow the cliff edge.
- Pass a trail to the right. (It leads to a dead end near the base of the water-fall.)
- Reach a "T," and turn right. (Left circles back to where you originally crossed the small creek.)
- Cross the small creek and climb to the abandoned railroad bed.
- Turn right, back onto the abandoned railroad bed.
- At 0.9 mile, there will be an observation deck to the right overlooking a waterfall.
- Continue downhill and cross under the green pipes.

- Reach a "T" near water level. Turn right (S).
- Pass old docks to the left.
- This trail dead ends at a cul-de-sac overlooking a cattail swamp area at 1.6 miles.
- Turn around and retrace your steps.
- Continue straight past the abandoned railroad bed to the left and an old road to the left.
- At 2.0 miles you can walk out on a dock into Turning Point Basin.
- After the dock, return to the old road and turn right (W) heading uphill.
- At the top of the hill, just before a silver metal gate, turn right (E) onto a dirt trail.
- Continue straight past a small paved trail. (It leads to a lookout to the right.)
- Quickly pass through a small trail intersection.
- At the "Y" bear right (E).
- At 2.4 miles pass a paved path to the left.
- The trail bends left. (Straight ahead is the second waterfall and a dead end at active railroad tracks.) Take a sharp left turn onto a paved path.
- At 2.6 miles reach a "Y" and bear right (SW).
- At 2.9 miles turn left on a dirt path. (Straight ends at Boxart Street.)
- Bear right past a trail to the left and continue to the parking area.

Date Hiked: _____

Notes:

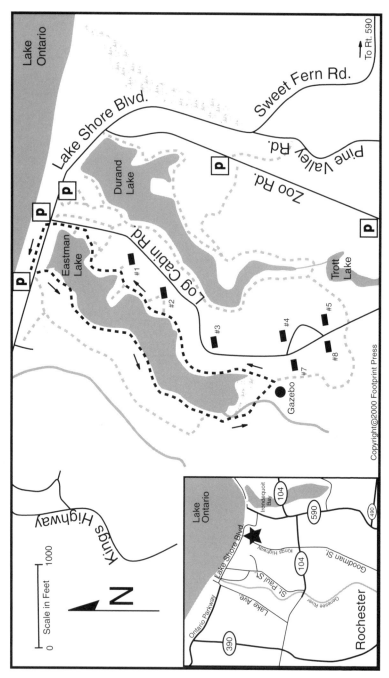

Eastman Lake Trail

54.
Eastman Lake Trail

Location: Durand Eastman Park, Rochester

Directions: Durand Eastman Park can be found along the shore of Lake Ontario, east of the Genesee River. Park in the parking area between Lake Shore Boulevard and Lake Ontario, near the northwest corner of Eastman Lake.

Alternative Parking: Along Log Cabin Road in Durand Eastman Park

Hiking Time: 1 hour

Length: 1.8 mile loop

Difficulty:

Surface: Dirt path

Trail Markings: None

Uses:

Dogs: OK on leash

Admission: Free

Contact: Monroe County Parks Department
171 Reservoir Avenue, Rochester, NY 14620
(716) 256-4950

Durand Eastman Park was a gift to the City of Rochester in 1908 from Dr. Henry Durand and George Eastman. It gave the city its first beachfront property and an opportunity for residents to explore the countryside outside the city's residential boundaries. Ownership passed to the County of Monroe in 1961.

Today the park is know mainly for its long sandy Lake Ontario beach, public golf course, and arboretum with herds of deer. During the winter the golf course becomes part of a network of cross-country ski trails. In summer, the trails are a bit more limited as golfers use their course. Still, a woods walk around Eastman Lake is a pleasure any time of year. It does require a 0.2 mile road walk to complete the loop.

Trail Directions
• From the parking area, cross Lake Shore Boulevard heading southeast.
• Enter the woods at the northwest corner of Eastman Lake. (Not on the mowed-grass area directly across from the parking area.)

215

- Pass some small trails off the main trail. The lake will appear to your left. Continue west along the edge of Eastman Lake.
- At 0.4 mile, pass a trail to the right. Continue straight (SW).
- At 0.6 mile, pass a cement structure.
- Just before reaching the golf course (mowed-grass) turn left (S) to cross some corduroy in a low, wet area.
- Reach a small creek at 0.7 mile. Bear right and follow the trail to the golf course.
- Turn left (SW) and cross the creek on a culvert along the edge of the golf course.
- Walk south along the edge of the golf course toward the gazebo.
- Enter the woods (E) on a trail just before the gazebo.
- Reach a "T" with a wide trail and turn left (N).
- Stay on the main trail. Several small trails will head off on both sides.
- The lake is now to your left.
- More small trails will lead off. Continue on the main trail along the lake.
- At 1.4 miles, pass a trail to the right that leads uphill to Shelter #1.
- Notice the large patch of Rhododendron on the hill to your right.
- At 1.5 miles, pass a trail to the right (It's a shortcut to Log Cabin Road.) Continue on the trail near the lake.
- Soon, turn left (E) on a narrower trail to stay near the lake.
- At a "T," turn right and head uphill to Log Cabin Road.
- Turn left (N) and follow the road toward Lake Ontario.
- At 1.7 mile, cross Lake Shore Boulevard. Turn left and follow the grass area along the road back to the parking area.

Date Hiked: _____

Notes:

Central
Section

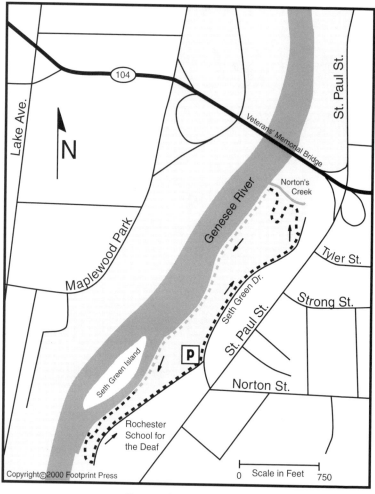

Seth Green Trail

55.
Seth Green Trail

Location:	Seth Green Drive, Rochester
Directions:	From Route 104, exit south on St. Paul Boulevard. Turn west on Seth Green Drive. Take the first left to find the parking area.

Alternative Parking: None

Hiking Time:	20 minutes round trip (official trail)
	40 minute loop (gorge loop trail)
Length:	0.9 mile round trip (official trail)
	1.4 mile loop (gorge loop trail)
Difficulty:	
Surface:	Dirt path, paved road
Trail Markings:	None
Uses:	
Dogs:	OK on leash
Admission:	Free
Contact:	Monroe County Parks Department
	171 Reservoir Avenue, Rochester, NY 14620
	(716) 256-4950

Two routes are described for the Seth Green Trail. The first is the official route which leads from the parking area to a switchbacked trail into the gorge and back out again. It follows a historic trail used by Native Americans for thousands of years. This trail offers a unique experience of the gorge as it descends past a dramatic rock face and waterfall below Seneca Towers and terminates at the river's edge.

The gorge loop trail uses maintained trails at either end of the loop but includes a 0.5-mile stretch of rough trail along the edge of the river which is nothing more than a path created by fishermen looking for a good casting spot. The loop is passable, but to follow it you have to expect some rough footing, downed trees, and overgrown bushes. It is easy to follow, with the river as your guide, but it is not a manicured trail. (This section is shown on the map as a grey trail.)

The land you'll walk is part of Seneca Park. The RG&E service road beyond the parking area leads to the base of the Lower Falls. In the early 1800s this area was home to the village of Carthage. It thrived as a steamboat landing and active mill site but was absorbed into Rochester upon its incorporation in 1834.

So, who was Seth Green? Adonijah Green ran a tavern at the corner of St. Paul and Norton Streets. His son Seth, born in 1817, spent many hours as a boy fishing, hunting, and trapping along the river. He observed the habits of fish. After running a successful fish and chowder business, he started the Caledonia Fish Hatchery. Seth Green received national and international fame as a fish grower and conservationist. The salmon stocked in the Genesee River today comes from the Caledonia Fish Hatchery.

The Veterans Memorial Bridge from within the Genesee River gorge.

Trail Directions — official trail (0.9 mile round trip)
• From the parking area, walk northeast along Seth Green Drive.
• In 0.2 mile, find a sign on the left that reads "This historic trail was used by Native Americans for thousands of years. Pioneer settlers expanded the trail and founded Carthage here in 1817." Turn left (W) and head downhill on the dirt trail.
• Follow the switchbacks downhill.
• View Norton's Creek waterfall at 0.3 mile.
• Continue downhill to water level at 0.4 mile. (This was once the site of Brewer's Landing.)
• To return, retrace your path uphill, then right along Seth Green Drive.

Trail Directions — gorge loop trail (1.4 mile loop)

Note: The gate at the far end of this loop is open from 6 AM to 7 PM daily. Do not begin this loop if it's after 6 PM. If you hear a loud siren or see flashing lights, do not proceed along the river's edge. This is a signal from the RG&E plant that means high water is approaching.

- From the parking area, walk northeast along Seth Green Drive.
- In 0.2 mile, find a sign on the left that reads "This historic trail was used by Native Americans for thousands of years. Pioneer settlers expanded the trail and founded Carthage here in 1817." Turn left (W) and head downhill on the dirt trail.
- Follow the switchbacks downhill.
- View Norton's Creek waterfall at 0.3 mile.
- Continue downhill to water level at 0.4 mile. (This was once the site of Brewer's Landing.)
- At river level, head left (SW) along the edge of the river. (For the next 0.5 mile the trail will be unmaintained.)
- Cross through a tire dumping ground.
- At 0.7 mile, pass an outflow drain.
- Continue along the river's edge through a rocky area. This requires some rock hopping.
- Pass Seth Green Island to the right.

The Lower Falls of the Genesee River.

- Pass a trail to the right and head uphill.
- At 1.1 mile, reach the paved RG&E service road and turn left, continuing uphill. (Notice the geologic layers in the bank to your right as you ascend.)
- Pass through the gate to the parking area. (The gate is open 6 AM to 7 PM daily.)

Date Hiked: _____

Notes:

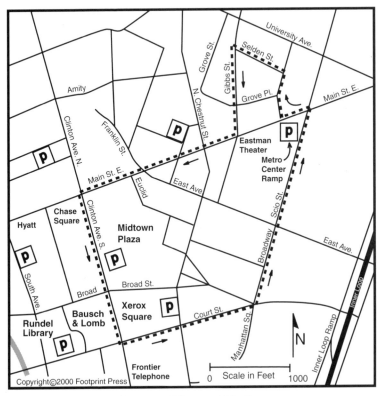

Grove Place Walk

56.
Grove Place Walk

Location: Theater District of downtown Rochester
Directions: Exit the Inner Loop on East Main Street. Turn left on
                   Scio Street and park in the Metro Center Ramp.
Alternative Parking: Numerous downtown parking ramps
Hiking Time: 45 minutes
Length: 1.2 mile loop
Difficulty:

Surface: Sidewalks
Trail Markings: Street signs
Uses:

Dogs: OK
Admission: Free
Information Furnished by:
                   American Heart Association
                   2113 Chili Avenue, Rochester, NY 14624
                   (716) 426-4050

   Enjoy a downtown stroll past quaint townhouses. Circle Midtown Plaza and Xerox Square on your tour of the best of downtown.

Trail Directions
• Exit the Metro Center Ramp Garage on Scio Street and head north.
• Turn left onto East Main Street.
• Pass Carpenter Alley then take a quick right (N) onto Windsor Street.
• Turn left (NW) at Selden Street and another left (S) onto Gibbs Street.
• At 0.4 mile, reach East Main Street. Turn right (W).
• Walk five blocks, and turn left onto Clinton Avenue at 0.6 mile.
• In two blocks turn left onto Court Street.
• In another two blocks turn left onto Broadway.
• Continue straight as Broadway becomes Scio Street, and return to the Metro Center Ramp Garage.

Date Hiked: _____
Notes:

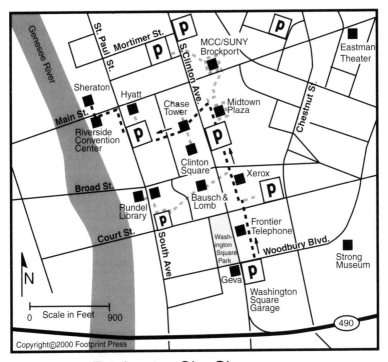

Rochester City Skyway

57.
Rochester City Skyway

Location: Downtown Rochester
Directions: Park in Washington Square Garage at the corner of
South Clinton Avenue and Woodbury Boulevard, near
Geva Theater
Alternative Parking: Several other downtown garages
Hiking Time: 45 minutes
Length: 1.3 miles round trip
Difficulty: ▓   (does involve stairs)

Surface: Every flooring type ever invented by man
Trail Markings: Blue Skyway logo signs
Uses:

Dogs: Pets are NOT allowed
Admission: Free
Contact :   City of Rochester
30 Church Street, Rochester, NY 14614
(716) 428-7000

OK, we all know there are days when the weather isn't quite the best in
Rochester. Don't let that stop you from walking. Try the indoor walkway in
downtown Rochester. This well-marked network of climate controlled
walkways, tunnels, and passageways connects a number of major downtown
buildings. It gives a bird's-eye view of downtown, its flavor and activities
through large windows. The Skyway is open 7 AM to 7 PM, Monday
through Saturday.

The Skyway takes you past the most recent developments of downtown
Rochester and through it's history as well. Midtown Plaza, built in 1959,
was the first indoor mall in a downtown area in the U.S. It was anchored by
the now defunct Sibleys and McCurdys department stores.

Trail Directions
• Leave Washington Square Garage at level 3 and follow the blue Skyway
logos through glassed-in walkways.
• At 0.2 mile, turn left and head upstairs (or take the escalator) toward
Xerox.
• At the top of the stairs, turn right then head down stairs.

- Continue straight at 0.3 mile, heading down stairs to Midtown Plaza. (Left leads for 0.3 mile, past Bausch & Lomb, through the South Avenue Parking Garage, to Rundel Library.)
- In Midtown Plaza, turn left (NE) and follow the Skyway signs.
- Turn left (W) at Scrantoms. (Right leads 0.2 mile through the old Sibley Building, which is now part of the MCC and SUNY Brockport campus, to the Mortimer Street garage)
- Enter Chase Bank.
- Take the escalator down 2 flights then turn right (W).
- At 0.5 mile, head down a ramp to a tunnel.
- Turn right, then left to head up the ramp.
- At 0.6 mile, reach South Avenue. Turn right and go up 2 escalator flights.

Graceful curves of the Rochester City Skyway.

- Follow signs into the Riverside Convention Center.
- Head down the escalator then bear left before the second escalator flight.
- At 0.7 mile, turn right (S) to cross the skybridge over Main Street. (Pause to enjoy the view of the Genesee River.)
- The Skyway ends in the Sheraton Hotel. Turn around and retrace your path back to the Washington Square Garage.

Date Hiked: _____

Notes:

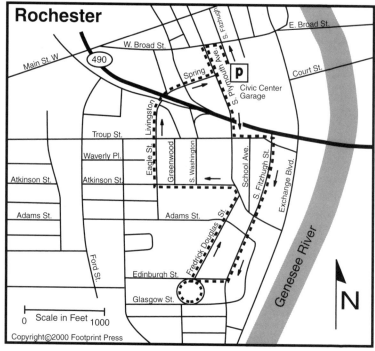

Corn Hill District Walk

58.
Corn Hill District Walk

Location: Corn Hill District of downtown Rochester

Directions: From Interstate 490, take the Plymouth Street exit. From Plymouth Street turn east on Broad Street then enter the Civic Center Garage across from South Fitzhugh Street.

Alternative Parking: Along the streets in Corn Hill

Hiking Time: 45 minutes

Length: 1.5 mile loop

Difficulty:

Surface: Sidewalks

Trail Markings: Street signs

Uses:

Dogs: OK

Admission: Free

Information Furnished by:
American Heart Association
2113 Chili Avenue, Rochester, NY 14624
(716) 426-4050

Step back in time as you wander through Corn Hill's neighborhood of restored homes. Before Nathaniel Rochester founded his name sake village in 1812, the Seneca Indians used this land for corn fields. Corn Hill was Rochester's first neighborhood, built in the early 1800s as flour-milling boomed.

Today Corn Hill is a vibrant neighborhood of mansions and workers cottages, restored to their original splendor. Among the buildings you'll find examples of Greek and Gothic Revival, Italian Villa, Second Empire, and Queen Anne houses.

Trail Directions
- Exit the Civic Center Garage to Broad Street and turn left (W) on Broad Street.
- Turn left onto South Plymouth Avenue.
- Cross over Interstate 490 and turn left (E) at the first street, onto Troup Street.

229

One of many restored homes in the Corn Hill District.

- Bear right on Fitzhugh Street and pass the Landmark Society headquarters.
- Continue straight, past South Plymouth Avenue and Adams Street.
- At 0.7 mile, turn right (W) on Edinburgh Street.
- When you come to Frederick Douglas Street turn left and walk around the circle with the gazebo in the center.
- Continue west on Frederick Douglas Street after completing the circle.
- Continue straight through a small park.
- At 1.1 mile, turn left on South Plymouth Avenue.
- Turn left onto Atkinson Street.
- At 1.3 mile, turn right (N) on Eagle Street.
- Continue straight on Livingston Park.
- Head toward the pedestrian bridge over Interstate 490.
- Bear right on Spring Street.
- At 1.4 mile, turn left on South Plymouth Avenue.
- At Broad Street turn right and return to the Civic Center Garage.

Date Hiked: _____

Notes:

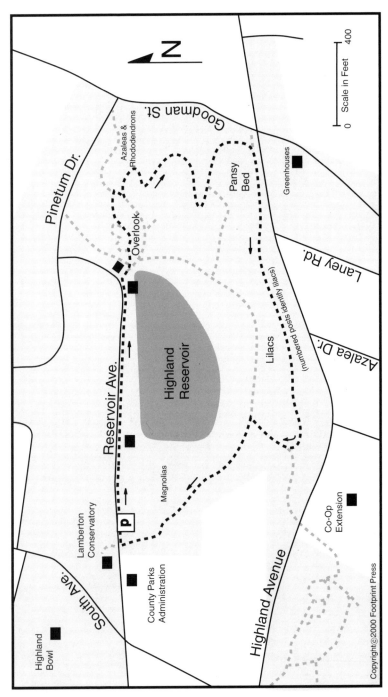

Lilac Trail

59.
Lilac Trail

Location:	Highland Park, Rochester
Directions:	Park along Reservoir Avenue, near Lamberton Conservatory

Alternative Parking: Any street near the Park.

Hiking Time:	40 minutes
Length:	1.3 mile loop
Difficulty:	👣 👣
Surface:	Paved and mowed-grass paths
Trail Markings:	Some signs
Uses:	🚶
Dogs:	OK on leash
Admission:	Free
Contact:	Monroe County Parks Department
	171 Reservoir Avenue, Rochester, NY 14620
	(716) 256-4950

Highland Park was Monroe County's first public park, dedicated in 1890 to the children of Rochester. The park began as a dream of two nursery-men, George Ellwanger and Patrick Barry who donated 20 acres of their nursery grounds to the city. Famous for its collections of magnolia, horse chestnut, barberry, Japanese maple, rhododendron, and lilac (more than 1,200), Highland Park is one of the oldest public arboretums or "tree gardens" in the United States.

Here are the best times to view various flowering plants:

mid-April	forsythia
late-April	magnolia
early-May	tulip
mid-May	flowering dogwood
late-May	azalea, lilac, pansy bed, wisteria
early-June	rhododendron
July	hydrangea

While enjoying the park, don't miss the Lamberton Conservatory, a landmark in Highland Park since 1911. Within the glass walls of the Conservatory, located on Reservoir Drive, are a wonderful tropical forest area, exotic plants, desert plants, plants with economic uses such as banana and coffee trees, and seasonal floral displays. Exhibits are changed five times throughout the year. The Conservatory hours are:

> May through October
> > Wednesday 10 AM to 8 PM
> > Thursday through Sunday 10 AM to 6 PM
> November through April
> > Wednesday through Sunday 10 AM to 4 PM
> > Closed Monday and Tuesday

The route described winds past the Highland Reservoir, and an overlook with a panoramic view of Rochester neighborhoods, then meanders downhill through the park. You'll pass the pansy bed then wind through the lilac grove. Numbered posts correspond to the descriptions below, giving you information on twenty varieties (within nine species) of lilacs. The final leg is uphill through the magnolia grove.

20. **Renoncule** (syringa vulgaris): This superior lilac is long-lived and bears large numbers of double lilac-colored flowers. One of the first developed by Victor Lemoine of France, the first horticulturist to cultivate lilacs.

19. **Rochester** (syringa vulgaris): Developed in Rochester, this was the first lilac to have more than four petals on a single floret (called radical doubling). The creamy-white flowers extend above dark-green glossy leaves.

18. **Primrose** (syringa vulgaris): Its outstanding pale-yellow color is not found in any other lilac. Developed in Holland in 1949.

17. **Hybrid** (syringa laciniata crossed with pinnatifolia): A cross between the Cutleaf lilac (#9) and the Pinnate lilac. The white flowers are flushed with purple and appear quite early. Notice the small, divided leaves.

16. **Znamya Lenina** (syringa vulgaris): Developed in Russia in 1963, one of the finest red-purple, single-flower lilacs.

15. **Frederick Law Olmsted** (syringa vulgaris): A Rochester hybrid named in 1987 after the designer of Highland Park. The abundant, single white flowers appear on a fairly dense shrub.

14. **Claude Bernard** (syringa hyacinthiflora): This Victor Lemoine selection blooms just before the common lilacs. The largest of the shrub lilacs, it produces double pinkish flowers with slightly twisted petals.

13. **President Lincoln** (syringa vulgaris): This hybrid was developed in 1916 by John Dunbar, the horticulturist who started Highland Park's lilac collection. It's one of the bluest lilacs, but new green foliage tends to hide the blossoms.

233

12. **Flower City** (syringa vulgaris): Developed in Rochester in 1983, has wonderful, single deep-purple blooms with numerous petals on a single flower. Underside of petals has a distinct silvery cast.

11. **Himalayan** (syringa emodi): Native to Afghanistan, this tall shrub has stout, gray branches and elliptical leaves.

10. **Cheyenne** (syringa oblata dilatata): Developed in 1971 and noted for its abundant, light-purple blooms and fine shrub shape. One of the few lilacs whose leaves turn orange in fall.

9. **Cutleaf** (syringa laciniata): A dense shrub native to northwestern China. Produces small, pale-purple tubular flowers early in May. The finely cut leaves are atypical of most lilacs.

8. **Rouen** (syringa chinensis): These large violet flower clusters produce a heavy fragrance that is most notable in high humidity. This flower is excellent for landscaping because it requires little maintenance.

7. **Corinne** (syringa vulgaris): A fine example of a magenta lilac, with somewhat open flower clusters. Developed in 1900 at the Baltet nursery in Troyes, France.

6. **Mademoiselle Casimer Perrier** (syringa vulgaris): A fine, white double flower developed in 1894 by Victor Lemoine.

5. **Frau Wilhelm Pfitzer** (syringa vulgaris): This large, vigorous lilac from Germany produces clusters of very fragrant, single pink flowers.

4. **Peking** (syringa pekinensis): One of only two lilac species that are small trees. This variety is native to northern China. Huge clusters of tiny creamy-white flowers bloom in mid-June. The soft green foliage, draping branches, and reddish-brown bark make this an attractive tree throughout the year.

3. **Handel** (syringa prestoniae): A large, vigorous shrub with fragrant, tubular pink flowers. Blooms about two weeks later than most lilacs. Isabel Preston of Ottawa, Canada, bred it in 1935 for the rugged climate of Canadian prairies, crossing two species native to China.

2. **Nokomis** (syringa hyacinthiflora): The single lilac-colored flower blooms slightly before the majority of the collection. Shrub developed in 1934 by Frank Skinner of Manitoba, Canada.

1. **Jessie Gardner** (syringa vulgaris): This fine American lilac produces abundant clusters of brilliant violet flowers growing on a rather large, rounded shrub.

Trail Directions

- From Lamberton Conservatory, walk east along Reservoir Avenue until you reach the old stone reservoir building (Gate House No.2) at 0.3 mile.

- Turn right on the paved walkway and immediately pass a trail to the left.
- Bear left at the next junction and head away from the reservoir.
- Bear right at the circle and pass the overlook area.
- At 0.5 mile, head down a flight of stairs and bear right. (Straight is a good side trip to take if the azaleas and rhododendrons are in bloom.)
- Make a sharp left turn and head downhill.
- Follow the paved path as it winds downhill.
- Bear left at the next junction.
- At the base of the hill, just before Highland Avenue, turn right and head west on the grass, parallel to Highland Avenue.
- Pass the pansy bed and continue west along a grass path through the numbered lilac bushes.
- Turn right (NE) when you meet the paved walkway at 1.2 miles and head uphill.
- At the next junction turn left (N) and pass through the magnolia grove. This walkway will take you back to Reservoir Avenue.

Date Hiked: _____

Notes:

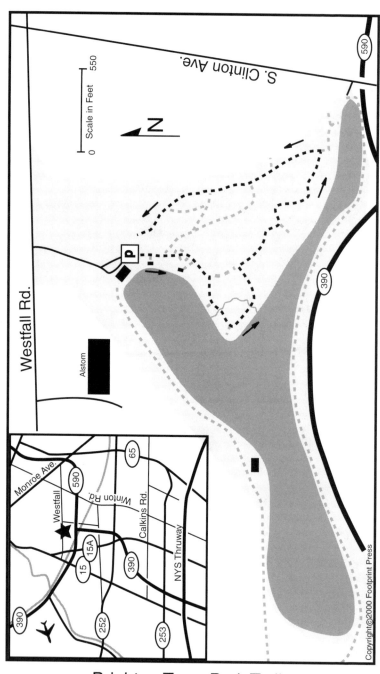

Brighton Town Park Trail

60.
Brighton Town Park Trail

Location:	Westfall Road, Brighton. Immediately north of the I-390/I-590 intersection.
Directions:	Brighton Town Park entrance is off Westfall Road, just west of South Clinton Avenue.

Alternative Parking: None
Hiking Time: 25 minutes
Length: 0.5 mile loop
Difficulty: 🥾🥾 🥾🥾

Surface: Dirt path
Trail Markings: None
Uses: 🚶 🎿

Dogs: OK on leash
Admission: Free
Contact: Brighton Recreation & Parks
220 Idlewood Road, Rochester, NY 14618
(716) 442-6585

Step into this beech forest and the noisy, busy world outside will disappear. You'll forget that the intersections of two busy highways are less than 0.5 mile away. The calm, quiet and cool, shade will envelop your mind and body to wash away stress. Such is the magic of this urban oasis.

If you're up for a more strenuous jaunt, walk the 1.3 mile loop around the retention pond. The trail is not maintained but a well-trodden path is available. Your serenade will be the whirr of traffic overhead and the honking of ducks and geese who live on the pond.

Trail Directions
- From the parking area, head south into the woods on a paved path.
- Continue straight (S) as the paved path bends right to a shelter.
- At the next 3 junctions, bear right (W). They come in quick succession.
- Reach a "T" at 0.1 mile and turn right (W).
- At the next junction, bear left(S). (Right is a short trail to a wood shed.)
- Turn right (W) at the next junction.
- Pass a short trail to the right, leading to the pond, then quickly cross a small wooden bridge.

- Pass several small trails to the right, leading to the pond. Continue on the main trail in the woods.
- At 0.2 mile, cross another small wooden bridge.
- Reach a "T" and turn right (S).
- Reach another "T" at 0.3 mile and turn left (E). (Right leads to a bench overlooking the pond.)
- Turn left (E) at the next "T." (Right leads to the pond.)
- Pass a trail to the right . (It's a dead end.)
- Continue straight (NE) passing two trails to the left.
- At the next junction, bear right (N).
- Continue straight until the trail emerges from the woods opposite the playground at the end of the parking area.

Date Hiked: _____

Notes:

Definitions

Arboretum: A tree garden where a variety of trees are planted and labeled for study and enjoyment.

Battery box: A box housing a battery as backup power for the railroad crossing gates and flashing lights in case of a power outage.

Blaze: A rectangular swath of paint used on trees to mark the path of a trail. (See picture on page 127.)

Corduroy: A method of spanning a wet section of trail by laying logs perpendicular to the trail. This creates a bumpy effect like corduroy material.

Deciduous: Describes trees that lose their leaves in winter.

Derecho: A fast-moving, long-lived storm that produces winds in excess of 58 miles per hour over a path of at least 280 miles in length. Commonly called a micro-burst, this storm can quickly fell many trees.

Drumlin: An elongated or oval hill created from glacial debris.

Esker: A ridge of debris formed when a river flowed under the glacier in an icy tunnel. Rocky material accumulated on the tunnel beds, and when the glacier melted, a ridge of rubble remained.

Feeder: A diverted stream, brook, or other water source used to maintain water level in a canal.

Fulling mill: A mill for cleaning wool and producing cloth.

Gorp: An abbreviation for "good old raisins and peanuts." It is used today to cover any combination of snacks taken to eat while hiking.

Gristmill: A mill for grinding grain into flour.

Guard gates: Large metal or wood and metal barriers which can be lowered into the canal to stop the flow of water.

Marsh: An area of soft, wet land.

Meromictic lake: A very deep body of water surrounded by high ridges. Because the high ridges prevent the wind from blowing on the water, a motionless surface gives the lake a mirrored effect.

Mule: The sterile offspring of a male donkey and a female horse. Mules were often used to pull boats along the Erie Canal.

Oxbow: A U-shaped bend in a river which eventually gets cut-off
                    from the main river and becomes a free-standing crescent
                    shaped body of water.

Quonset hut: A trademark used for a prefabricated portable hut having
                    a semicircular roof of corrugated metal that curves down
                    to form walls.

Riparian zone: Land located on the bank of a natural waterway.

Sawmill: A mill for cutting trees into lumber.

Swamp: Wet, spongy land saturated and sometimes partially or
                    intermittently covered with water.

Switchbacks: Winding the trail back and forth across the face of a steep
                    area to make the incline more gradual.

Trestle: A framework consisting of vertical, slanted supports and
                    horizontal crosspieces supporting a bridge. This con-
                    struction is often used for railroad bridges.

Waste weir: A dam along the side of the canal which allows overflow
                    water to dissipate into a side waterway.

Trails Under 1.2 Miles

Trails 1.2 to 1.5 Miles

Trails 1.6 to 2.3 Miles

Trails 1.6 to 2.3 Miles

Page	Trail Name	Length (miles)
180	Lost City of Tryon Trail (loop)	1.7
63	Tinker Nature Park Perimeter + Nature Trails (loop)	1.7
214	Eastman Lake Trail	1.8
110	Earth is Our Mother Trail (loop)	1.9
39	Northampton Ski Loop (loop)	2.0
55	Plaster Woods Trail (loop)	2.0
138	Indian Hill Section (loop)	2.1
177	Coyotes Den Trail (loop)	2.1
28	Greece Canal Park Trail (loop)	2.2
69	Genesee Valley Greenway - Rochester (one way)	2.2
99	Royal Coach Trail (loop)	2.2
141	Cartersville - Great Embankment Loop Trail (loop)	2.2
152	Horizon Hill Section (loop)	2.2
83	Devil's Bathtub Trail (loop)	2.3

Trails 2.4 to 5.0 Miles

Page	Trail Name	Length (miles)
195	Bay Trail (round trip)	2.4
45	Hardwood Swamp Trail (loop)	2.5
89	Quaker Pond Trail (loop)	2.5
172	Thousand Acre Swamp Trail (loop)	2.6
149	McCoord Woods Section (loop)	2.8
129	Fish Hatchery + Old Ski Run Trails (loop)	2.8
195	Bay Trail (round trip)	3.0
209	Turning Point Park & Bullocks Wood Preserve (loop)	3.0
45	Hardwood Swamp + Black Creek Field Trails (loop)	3.3
28	Greece Canal Park + Farm Artifact Trails (loop)	3.3
96	Mendon Grasslands Trail (loop)	3.4
123	Daffodil Trail (loop)	3.4
183	Old Rifle Range Trail (loop)	3.4
50	Genesee Country Nature Center (loop)	3.5
86	Birdsong + Quaker Pond Trails (loop)	3.6
42	Black Creek Trail (loop)	4.2
202	Olmsted/Seneca Trail (round trip)	4.3
69	Genesee Valley Greenway - Rochester (round trip)	4.4
123	Daffodil + Irondequoit Creek Trails (loop)	4.5
149	McCoord Woods + Horizon Hill Trails (loop)	5.0

Trails More Than 5 Miles

Page	Trail Name	Length (miles)
145	Historic Erie Canal & Railroad Loop Trail (loop)	5.3
91	Eastern Ski Trail (loop)	5.7
89	Quaker Pond + Mendon Grasslands Trails (loop)	5.9
113	Seneca Trail (one way)	5.8
72	Genesee Valley Greenway - Scottsville (one way)	6.6
91	Eastern Ski Trail + Pine Forest Loop (loop)	6.9
42	Black Creek + Hardwood Swamp Trails (loop)	6.7
24	Genesee River Trail (round trip)	7.0
191	Webster Hojack Trail (round trip)	8.2
24	Genesee River Trail + Turning Point Park (one way)	8.5
74	Genesee Valley Greenway - Scottsville (one way)	8.4
113	Seneca Trail (round trip)	11.6
72	Genesee Valley Greenway - Scottsville north (round trip)	13.2
72	Genesee Valley Greenway - Scottsville south (round trip)	16.8
69	Genesee Valley Greenway - Rochester to Avon (one way)	18.9

Contains a Wheelchair Accessible Segment

1 Boot Trails

2 Boot Trails

2 Boot Trails

3 Boot Trails

4 Boot Trails

Trails to Waterfalls

Educational Trails

Historical Trails

Trails for Horseback Riding

Trails for Bicycle Riding

Trails for Cross-Country Skiing

The authors, Rich and Sue Freeman decided to make their living from what they love — hiking and bicycling. In 1996 they left corporate jobs to spend six months hiking 2,200 miles on the Appalachian Trail from

Georgia to Maine. That adventure deepened their love of the outdoors and inspired them to share this love by introducing others to the joys of hiking. Since most people don't have the option (let alone the desire) to undertake a six-month trek, they decided to focus on short hikes, near home. The result was the first version of *Take A Hike! Family Walks in the Rochester Area.* They went on to explore hiking and bicycling trails throughout the central and western New York State region.

Rich and Sue have been active members of Victor Hiking Trails since its inception. They continue to do trail work and participate with other local trail groups as well. In addition, their passion for long distance hiking continues. In 1997 they thru-hiked the 500-mile long Bruce Trail in Ontario, Canada. In 1998 they bicycled across New York State, following the Erie Canalway Trail and 1999 found them hiking a segment of the Florida Trail.

Since beginning their new career writing and publishing books, the Freeman's have pared down their living expenses and are enjoying a simpler lifestyle. They now have control of their own destiny and the freedom to head into the woods for a refreshing respite when the urge strikes. Still, their life is infinitely more cluttered than when they carried all their worldly needs on their backs for six months on the Appalachian Trail.

Take Your Bike! Family Rides in the Rochester Area
  ISBN# 0-9656974-28   U.S. $16.95
  Converted railroad beds, paved bike paths, woods trails, and
  little used country roads combine to create the 30 safe bicycle
  adventures within an easy drive of Rochester, N.Y. No need to
  have a mountain bike – any sturdy bicycle will do.

Take A Hike! Family Walks in the Finger Lakes & Genesee Valley Region
  ISBN# 0-9656974-95   U.S. $16.95
  Perfect for an afternoon walk, ramble, or hike on 51 trails
  through forests, glens, and bogs of upstate N.Y. Each trail has a
  map, description, and details you'll need such as where to park,
  estimated hiking time, and interesting points along the way.

Take Your Bike! Family Rides in the Finger Lakes & Genesee Valley Region
  ISBN# 0-9656974-44   U.S. $16.95
  Converted railroad beds, paved bike paths, woods trails, and
  little used country roads combine to create the 40 safe bicycle
  adventures through central and western N.Y. No need to have a
  mountain bike – any sturdy bicycle will do.

Bruce Trail – An Adventure Along the Niagara Escarpment
  ISBN# 0-9656974-36   U.S. $16.95
  Join experienced backpackers on a five-week journey along the
  Niagara Escarpment in Ontario, Canada. Explore the now abandoned Welland Canal routes, caves formed by crashing waves,
  ancient cedar forests, and white cobblestone beaches along azure
  Georgian Bay. Learn the secrets of long-distance backpackers. As
  an armchair traveler or in preparation for a hike of your own,
  enjoy this ramble along a truly unique part of North America.

Peak Experiences – Hiking the Highest Summits of New York,
  County by County
  ISBN# 0-9656974-01   U.S. $16.95
  Bag the highest point in each of the 62 counties of New York
  State with this often amusing guidebook. Some are barely mole
  hills that can be driven by, others are significant mountain peaks
  that require a good day's climb. All promise the exhilaration of
  new discoveries.

Alter – A Simple Path to Emotional Wellness
  ISBN# 0-9656974-87   U.S. $16.95
  Alter is a self-help manual which assists in recognizing and
  changing your emotional blocks and limiting belief systems. It
  uses easy-to-learn techniques of biofeedback to retrieve sublimi-
  nal information and achieve personal transformation.

For sample maps and chapters explore web site:
http://www.footprintpress.com

Yes, I'd like to order Footprint Press books:

#

_____ *Peak Experiences - Hiking the Summits of NY Counties* $16.95

_____ *Take A Hike! Family Walks in the Rochester Area* $16.95

_____ *Take A Hike! Family Walks in the Finger Lakes* $16.95

_____ *Take Your Bike! Family Rides in the Rochester Area* $16.95

_____ *Take Your Bike! Family Rides in the Finger Lakes* $16.95

_____ *Bruce Trail - Adventure Along the Niagara Escarpment* $16.95

_____ *Backpacking Trails of Central & Western NYS* $2.00

_____ *Alter – A Simple Path to Emotional Wellness* $16.95

Sub-total $_____

NYS and Canadian residents add 8% tax $_____

Shipping is FREE

Total enclosed: $_____

Your Name: _____

Address: _____

City: _____ State (Province): _____

Zip (Postal Code): _____ Country: _____

Make check payable and mail to:
Footprint Press
P.O. Box 645
Fishers, N.Y. 14453

Or, check the web site at http://www.footprintpress.com

Footprint Press books are available at special discounts
when purchased in bulk for sales promotions,
premiums, or fund raising.